D0869321

The Aquinas Lecture, 1993

PERSON AND BEING

Under the auspices of the
Wisconsin-Alpha Chapter of Phi Sigma Tau

by

W. NORRIS CLARKE, S.J.

Marquette University Press
Milwaukee
1993

Library of Congress Catalogue Number: 92-63402

Copyright 1993

Marquette University Press

ISBN 0-87462-160-7

Prefatory

The Wisconsin-Alpha Chapter of Phi Sigma Tau, the National Honor Society for Philosophy at Marquette University, each year invites a scholar to deliver a lecture in honor of St. Thomas Aquinas.

The 1993 Aquinas Lecture, *Person and Being*, was delivered in the Tony and Lucille Weasler Auditorium of the Alumni Memorial Union on Sunday, February 28, 1993, by the Reverend W. Norris Clarke, S.J., Professor Emeritus of Philosophy at Fordham University, The Bronx, New York, and Visiting Professor of Philosophy at Xavier Unversity, Cincinnati, Ohio.

Fr. Clarke was born in New York City and attended Georgetown University before entering the Society of Jesus. He began his study of philosophy at the Collège Saint Louis on the Isle of Jersey and then earned an M.A. in philosophy at Fordham University before doing his theological studies at Woodstock College, Woodstock, Maryland, and earning his Ph.D. at the University of Louvain in 1950. Fr. Clarke taught philosophy at Fordham University from 1955 to 1985, becoming professor of philosophy in 1968 and professor emeritus in 1985. Since his retirement from Fordham University, he has been visiting professor at Santa Clara University, Villanova University, Xavier University, Wheeling Jesuit

College, Canisius College, and Immaculate Conception Seminary at Seton Hall University.

Fr. Clarke was co-founder and editor-in-chief of the *International Philosophical Quarterly* from 1961 to 1985. He has been president of the American Catholic Philosophical Association, the Metaphysical Society of America, and the Jesuit Philosophical Association. He received the Aquinas Medal from the American Catholic Philosophical Association in 1980 for his distinguished contribution to Christian philosophy. He received the Outstanding Teacher Award from Fordham University and received an honorary degree from Villanova University.

Fr. Clarke is the author of two books, *The Philosophical Approach to God: A Contemporary Neo-Thomist Perspective* (1979) and *The Universe as Journey* (1988). He has published over fifty articles and chapters in books. Among his more recent publications are: "Is a Natural Theology Still Possible Today?" "Charles Hartshone's Philosophy of God: A Thomistic Critique," "Thomism and Contemporary Philosophical Pluralism," "The 'We Are' of Interpersonal Dialogue as the Starting Point of Metaphysics," and "To Be Is To Be Substance-in-Relation."

To Fr. Clarke's distinguished list of publications, Phi Sigma Tau is pleased to add *Person and Being*.

PERSON AND BEING

by

W. NORRIS CLARKE, S.J.

Contents

PERSON AND BEING

Introduction

Many of you who will hear or read this lecture are already familiar, I gather, with some of my work on the metaphysics of St. Thomas Aquinas (the themes of participation, action, etc.). But in recent years I have been focusing my attention more on the human person in St. Thomas and its links with his metaphysics of being. So I am delighted to be offered this distinguished and widely respected forum to gather together in one place the ideas that I have been putting forth piecemeal elsewhere.

My objective in this present lecture is to present for your reflection and criticism what I would call a "creative retrieval and completion" of St. Thomas's own thought on the metaphysics of the person, in particular the human person. My own endeavour here is actually part of a loose, ongoing cooperation that has recently been developing among a growing number of Thomistic thinkers, some philosophers, some theologians, who feel the need, as I do, to draw out and highlight a dynamic and relational notion of person which seems to us clearly implied in St. Thomas's own metaphysics of being as existential act, but

was never quite made explicit by Thomas himself
in his philosophical analysis of the person.[1]

One of the stimuli for this line of thought has
been the challenge laid down some years ago by
Cardinal Josef Ratzinger (in what I might call his
earlier incarnation as a creative, even daring,
theologian), namely, that Christian thinkers had
developed a relational notion of the person for
use in theology, to help explain the Trinity of
three Persons united in one God, but had not
exploited it adequately, if at all, in their
philosophical analyses of the person. He explicitly
reproaches St. Thomas himself for this, and calls
for a new, explicitly relational conception of the
very nature of the person as such, wherein relationality would become an equally primordial
aspect of the person as substantiality. To quote
him:

> [In the relational notion of person devel-
> oped within the theology of the Trin-
> ity] . . . lies concealed a revolution in man's
> view of the world: the undivided sway of
> thinking in terms of substance is ended;
> relation is discovered as an equally valid
> primordial mode of reality . . . and it is
> made apparent how being that truly under-
> stands itself grasps at the same time that *in*
> its self-being it does not belong to itself;
> that it only comes to itself by moving away

from itself and finding its way back as
relatedness to its true primordial state.[2]

A similar criticism of the lack of carry-over
from the theological notion of person to the
philosophical by St. Thomas has also been made
by Karol Wojtyla (now Pope John Paul II) in his
philosophical writings on the person. I think the
two cardinals do have a point. Yet just such a
dynamic, relational notion of the person seems to
me – and to others now working along the same
lines – already implicit, waiting just under the
surface to be developed, in Thomas's own highly
dynamic notion of existential being (*esse*) as act
and as intrinsically ordered toward self-communication. St. Thomas himself did not develop this
aspect explicitly, possibly because he did not have
the time or the urgent occasion to do so. The
immediate central focus of the metaphysical
analysis of the person in university circles at his
time was on how to explain the distinction
between person and nature and how to identify
the root of the "incommunicability" or uniqueness
of each person as distinct from the common nature they shared: natures could be shared,
personhood not. It is precisely such a creative
completion (or "retrieval," as Heidegger would
say) of this underdeveloped dimension of St.
Thomas's metaphysics of the person that I would
like to present to you here. But, since Thomas

himself did not explicitly work out this aspect of his thought, I must take my own responsibility for what follows, except for the basic inspiration I have received from his own inexhaustibly seminal thinking.

There is another urgent reason for undertaking this "creative completion" today. The second part of our century has seen a rich development of the relational aspects of the person, worked out by existential phenomenologists and personalists of various schools, as well as by schools of psychology and psychotherapy, extending from Heidegger to Sartre, Gabriel Marcel, Emmanuel Mounier and the French personalists, Martin Buber, Levinas, John Macmurray, Viktor Frankl, and many others. St. Thomas himself would have been delighted, I think, with these rich phenomenological analyses of our own time, since this aspect of his own thought was usually only very sketchily developed. Yet these valuable analyses have almost without exception been suspicious of, or even positively hostile towards the notion of person as *substance*, which was so heavily stressed in the classical tradition – ancient, medieval, and early modern. As a result, the being of the person has been explained so onesidedly in terms of relation and systems of relations that the dimension of the person as abiding self-identity, interiority, and in-itselfness has tended to disappear from sight, or at least lose all metaphysical grounding.

Hence we are faced, on the one hand, with a rich older metaphysical tradition of the person that has left the relational dimension underdeveloped and, on the other, with a more recent phenomenological tradition that has highly developed the relational aspect but lost its metaphysical grounding. What is urgently needed is a creative integration of these two valuable but incomplete lines of thought into a more complete and well-rounded philosophy of the person. What I hope to do is to make a start on this integration by grafting the self-communicative, relational dimension of the person right onto the Thomistic metaphysics of being as existential, self-communicative act, showing how it is already in principle implicit therein. I propose to do this by developing the dynamic, relational aspect of being itself for St. Thomas, with its indissoluble complementarity of substantiality, the *in-itself* dimension of being, and relationality, the *towards-others* aspect. Then I will apply this dyadic structure to the person as the highest manifestation of being itself, with the resulting characteristics of the person as self-possessing, self-communicative, and self-transcending.

I. Being as Dynamic Act

1. Being as Active and Self-Communicative

One of the central themes in the thought of Aquinas is his notion of real being, i.e., actually existing being, as intrinsically active and self-communicating. A superficial reading of him might not notice this at first, because it is never thematized as the formal question asked in any question or article. But it runs all through his thought, both philosophical and theological, as one of the key mediating ideas in explanations and drawing of conclusions, as I have tried to show at greater length in my article on the subject.[3] A sampling of his texts will show this clearly enough.

> From the very fact that something exists in act, it is active.[4]

> Active power follows upon being in act, for anything acts in consequence of being in act.[5]

> It is the nature of every actuality to communicate itself insofar as it is possible. Hence every agent acts according as it exists in actuality.[6]

It follows upon the superabundance proper to perfection as such that the perfection which something has it can communicate to another. Communication follows upon the very intelligibility (*ratio*) of actuality. Hence every form is of itself communicable.[7]

For natural things have a natural inclination not only toward their own proper good, to acquire it, if not possessed, and if possessed, to rest therein; but also to diffuse their own goodness among others as far as is possible. Hence we see that every agent, insofar as it exists in act and possesses some perfection, produces something similar to itself. It pertains, therefore, to the nature of the will to communicate to others as far as possible the good possessed; and especially does this pertain to the divine will, from which all perfection is derived in some kind of likeness. Hence if natural things, insofar as they are perfect, communicate their goodness to others, much more does it pertain to the divine will to communicate by likeness its own goodness to others as far as possible.[8]

Not only is activity, active self-communication, the natural consequence of possessing an act of existence (*esse*); St. Thomas goes further to maintain that self-expression through action is actually the whole point, the natural perfection or flowering of being itself, the goal of its very presence in the universe:

> Every substance exists for the sake of its operation.[9]

> Each and every thing shows forth that it exists for the sake of its operation; indeed, operation is the ultimate perfection of each thing.[10]

Thus there is an immense innate dynamism in the very nature of actual being as such – wherever an act of existing is found, participated or unparticipated – to pour over into self-expression, self-communication of its own inner perfection or goodnesss. Full credit must be given to Etienne Gilson for his role in rediscovering the centrality and dynamism of the act of existence in contemporary Thomism. As he puts it pithily:

> Not: to be, then to act, but: to be is to act. And the very first thing which "to be" does, is to make its own essence to be, that is, "to be a being." This is done at once, completely and definitively. . . . But the next thing which "to be" does, is to begin bringing its own individual essence somewhat nearer its own completion.[11]

Gerald Phelan, one of the early disciples of Gilson at Toronto, was also peculiarly sensitive to the expansive character of being through action:

> The act of existence (*esse*) is not a state, it is an act, the act of all acts, and therefore must be understood as act and not as a static definable object of conception. *Esse* is dynamic impulse, energy, act – the first, the most persistent and enduring of all dynamisms, all energies, all acts. In all things on earth, the act of being (*esse*) is the consubstantial urge of nature, a restless, striving force, carrying each being (*ens*) forward, from within the depths of its own reality to its full self-achievement.[12]

Despite their sensitivity to the intrinsic connection between *to be* and *to act*, these comments of Gilson and Phelan limit their focus to the drive of each being towards fulfilling its own perfection, to its passage from its own potency to its own act – still in some respects an Aristotelian perspective. Aquinas, in the texts we have seen above, goes considerably further, speaking of an intrinsic dynamism in every being to be *self-communicative*, to share its own goodness with others, to pour over into production of another actuality in some way like itself. This is what Maritain has aptly called "the basic generosity of existence."[13] The

principal credit for retrieving this self-communicative aspect of being must be given to
Joseph de Finance for his seminal book, *Etre et
agir*, unfortunately never put into English.[14]

It follows that, for Aquinas, finite, created
being pours over naturally into action for *two* rea-
sons: (1) because it is *poor*, i.e., lacking the fullness of existence, and so strives to enrich itself as
much as its nature allows from the richness of
those around it; but (2) even more profoundly
because it is *rich*, endowed with its own richness
of existence, however slight this may be, which it
tends naturally to communicate and share with
others.

This innate fecundity and generosity proper
to being as existent, by which it is naturally self-
communicating to others, is St. Thomas's way of
integrating into his own metaphysics of being the
rich Platonic and Neoplatonic tradition of the self-
diffusiveness of the Good (understood as more
ultimate than being, since for both Plato and
Plotinus "being" always meant limited intelligible
essence). Existence itself (*esse*) now becomes for
Thomas the ultimate root of all perfection, with
unity and goodness its transcendental properties
or attributes, facets of the inexhaustible richness
of being itself. And once the Platonic realism of
ideas is overcome, which forbade the location of
these ideas – as multiplied – within the supreme

One itself, Thomas's Supreme Being, the pure subsistent Act of Existence, can now become identically intelligence and will, and the intrinsic self-diffusiveness of the Good turns into personal love, self-communicative love.

The ultimate reason now appears why all beings, by the very fact that they *are*, possess this natural dynamism toward self-communicative action: they are all diverse modes of participation in the infinite goodness of the one Source, whose very being is self-communicative love. So much could be reached, dimly at least, by a reflective integration of the Aristotelian and Neoplatonic traditions. But Christian philosophy, drawing upon God's own self-revelation in the doctrine of the Trinity (three Persons within one Divine Being) can here illumine the very nature of being, as well as of God, in a way far beyond the grasp of human reason left to itself. For what the doctrine of the Trinity means is that the very inner nature of the Supreme Being itself – even before its overflow into creation – is an ecstatic process (beyond time and change) of self-communicating love: the Father, unoriginated possessor of the infinite fullness of the divine nature, communicates ecstatically his entire divine nature to the Second Person, the Son or the Word, in an act of loving self-knowledge, so that the only distinction between them is the distinction of two complementary but opposed relations, Giver and Receiver. Then both together, in a single act of mutual love, pour forth the same divine essence again in all its fullness to their love image, the Holy Spirit, the third Person. Thus the very inner life of God himself, the supreme fullness of what it means to be, is by its very nature *self-communicative Love*, which then subsequently flows over freely in the finite self-communication that is creation. No wonder, then, that self-communication is written into the very heart of all beings, as finite but positive images of their Source. Philosophy and revelation here go hand in hand to open up the profoundest depths of what it means to be.

This understanding of being as intrinsically active, self-manifesting, and self-communicating I consider not merely as a position of historical interest for understanding ancient and medieval thought, but also in its own right as one of the few great fundamental insights in the history of metaphysics, without which no viable metaphysical vision of the universe can get far off the ground. For consider what would happen if one attempted to deny that every real being is active, self-manifesting through action. Suppose a being that really exists, but does not act in any way, does not manifest itself in any way to other beings. There would be no way for anything else to know that it exists; it would make no *difference* at all to the rest of reality; practically speaking, it might just as well not be at all – it would in fact be indistinguishable from non-being. If many or all real beings were this way, each would be locked off in total isolation from every other. There would not be a connected universe (its root, *universum*, means in fact "turned toward unity"). The only way that beings can connect up with each other to form a unified system is through action. To be and to be active, though conceptually distinct, are inseparable. "Communication," as Aquinas says, "follows upon the very intelligibility of actuality." The full meaning of "to be" is not just "to be *present*," but "to be *actively present*." Existence is power-full, energy-filled presence. *Agere sequitur esse* (action follows upon being, as the medieval adage has it, although the interpretation varied according to the meaning given to *esse*). To know another being, therefore, is to know it as *this kind of actor*, on me or others, as manifested to me.[15]

2. Being as Relational

The innate dynamism of being as overflowing into self-manifesting, self-communicating action is clear and explicit in St. Thomas, if one knows where to look. Not as explicit, however, though necessarily implied, it seems to me, is the corollary that *relationality* is a primordial dimension of every real being, inseparable from its substantiality, just as action is from existence. For if a being naturally flows over into self-communicating action toward others, and also receives from them, then it cannot help but generate a network of relations with all its recipients. Action, "passion" (being acted upon), and relations are inseparably linked up together even in the Aristotelian categories. While all relations are not generated by action, still all action and passion necessarily generate relations.

It turns out, then, that relationality and substantiality go together as two distinct but inseparable modes of reality. Substance is the primary mode, in that all else, including relations, depend on it as their ground. But since "every substance exists for the sake of its operations," as St. Thomas has just told us, being as substance, as existing *in itself*, naturally flows over into being as relational, as turned *towards others* by its self-communicating action. *To be* fully is to be *substance-in-relation*.[16]

Aquinas does indeed call the act of existence by which a being is present in itself, as standing out of nothingness, the "first act" of the being, and the action or operation proceeding from it, which grounds its relationality, its "second act." There is indeed a priority of dependence here: the second act is rooted in and flows from the first.

But this does not mean that this second act is secondary in importance, or purely accidental in the sense that the being could be a real being whether it expresses itself in action or not. On the contrary, the second act is the very goal and fulfillment in being of the first act, its ultimate *raison d'être*. Relationality is, therefore, in principle for St. Thomas himself, an equally primordial dimension of being as substantiality. Let us say so explicitly.

In a creature it may well be accidental *which* particular other being it will be related to here and now. But *being related* in some way to the world around it, as well as to its various sources, will flow from its very nature both as existent being and as material. Within the divine being, the relations of procession between the three Persons are not accidental but constitutive of the very nature of the divine substance. Substantiality and relationality are here equally primordial and necessary dimensions of being itself at its highest intensity. And the ultimate reason why all lower beings manifest this relationality as well as substantiality is that they are all in some way images of God, their ultimate Source, the supreme synthesis of both. All being, therefore, is, by its very nature as being, *dyadic*, with an "introverted," or *in-itself* dimension, as substance, and an "extraverted," or *towards-others* dimension, as related through action.

Even though we have been stressing the relational aspect of being so far in this discussion, since it was underdeveloped in the Aristotelian-Thomistic tradition, it should not be forgotten that the aspect of substantiality, already well developed in this tradition, is indispensable, as the necessary grounding for relationality itself. For the very meaning of relation implies that it is *between* two terms that it is connecting, between two relat*eds*. A relation cannot relate nothing. Thus a relat*ed* is not simply identical with its rela*tion*, reducible to it without remainder; it is distinct from it though not separable from it (as related). No relation can be self-supporting by itself. If what it relates is itself a relation, then we must look further for a grounding of that, and there cannot be an infinite regress here. There must be an *in-itself* somewhere along the line to ground the betweenness. This is the ontological role of substance in a being: to provide the abiding unifying center for all the being's relations and other attributes. This aptness to *exist in itself*, not as a part of any other being (the classical definition of substance), is what makes a being, in Bernard Lonergan's words, to be "a unity-identity-whole," a unity-whole now in all its parts and identical down through time. This is too often forgotten by contemporary phenomenologists and personalists who tend to stress so exclusively the person as constituted by its relations to others that the inner depth and interiority of the person tend to get swallowed up in its extraverted relationships. The inseparable complementarity of *in-itself* and *towards-others* must be maintained: to be is to be *substance-in-relation*.

Contemporary Western thinkers are not always aware of the metaphysical trap laid long ago by the Buddhists for those who would reduce the world of multiplicity we live in to nothing but relations. For if, they rightly argue, A is nothing but a relation to B, and reciprocally B is nothing but a relation to A, and so of all things, so that all is but a web of pure relations, then nothing has "own-being," as they say, and all fall together into emptiness (*sunyatta*); only the non-related, unlimited, and unchanging can be really real (*Nirvana*), and it cannot be spoken about. The Buddhists themselves rejoice in this conclusion (having already gotten rid of substance by the classic Humean-type argument that whatever is distinct is separable, and a substance separated from all relations would be at once unrelated yet still related). But it is not at all clear that anti-substance Western thinkers would be happy to see their whole empirical world dissolve thus into the void.

Let us conclude this section with a quotation from Josef Pieper, who, more than most contemporary Thomists, has brought out the proportional connection between the two aspects of being:

> To sum it up, then: to have (or to be) an "intrinsic existence" means "to be able to relate" and "to be the sustaining subject at the center of a field of reference." Only in reference to an inside can there be an outside. Without a self-contained "subject" there can be no "object." Relating-to, conforming-with, being-oriented-toward – all these notions presuppose an inside starting point. . . . The higher the form of intrinsic existence, the more developed becomes the relatedness to reality, also the more profound and comprehensive becomes the sphere of this relatedness: namely, the world. And the deeper such relations penetrate the world of reality, the more intrinsic becomes the subject's existence.[17]

This dynamic polarity between substance and action-plus-relations got submerged and almost forgotten in the post-medieval period from Descartes on. Three major distortions of the classical notion of substance broke the connection: (1) the Cartesian notion of the isolated, unrelated substance, "that which needs nothing else but itself (and God) to exist"; (2) the Lockean static substance, the inert substratum needed to support accidents but unknowable in itself; and (3) the separable substance of Hume, which, if it existed, would have to be empirically observable as separated from all its accidents, and hence is an impossible fiction.

Because these emasculated versions of substance were the only ones familiar to them from classical modern philosophy, a large number of modern and contemporary thinkers have simply rejected substance entirely as a nonviable mode of being, e.g., Bergson, Collingwood, Whitehead, Dewey, Heidegger, most phenomenologists (Sartre, Marcel, etc.), and many others. As a result, the person tends to be reduced to nothing but a relation or set of relations. The difficulty here, however, as Pieper warned, is that if the substance, or *in-itself*, pole of being is dropped out, the unique interiority and privacy of the person are wiped out also and the person turns out to be an entirely extraverted bundle of relations, with no inner self to share with others. But there is no need for this either/or dichotomy between substance and relation, once the notion of substance as center of activity – and receptivity – has been retrieved.

3. Being as Receptivity, Community, Communion

This section, like the preceding one on rationality, is an explicit thematizing of what is implied in the Thomistic understanding of being as dynamic and self-communicative. Once the latter point has been established, several corollaries follow necessarily from it.

1) If self-communication is a fundamental aspect of real being, so too must be *receptivity*, the complementary pole of self-communication. Without receptivity no communication can become actual and complete itself. It must therefore be a primordial dimension of reality as a whole, even though it follows upon the substantial and self-communication aspects of being in the ontological (not necessarily temporal) order of dependence and intelligibility.

Another important consequence follows, one habitually overlooked or underdeveloped in the classical tradition, including the Thomistic. Receptivity as such should be looked on not as essentially a sign of imperfection, of poverty, of potentiality in the receiver, as we have tended to look on it, but as in itself a positive aspect or *perfection* of being. Without it love, authentic mutual love, would necessarily remain incomplete – and love is of itself a purely positive perfection. In the lower levels of being, indeed, receptivity is woven in with poverty, incompleteness, the process of change from potentiality to actuality. As we move higher in the scale of being, however, specifically into the personal, it turns more and more into an active, welcoming, gratefully responsive attitude, which is a positive, joy-bringing aspect of personal relations. And if all change and time is removed from it, so that the receiver always possesses what it has as gift, as in the case of the inner life of the divine Persons in the Christian Trinity, then receptivity, represented archetypically by the Second Person as Son and Word, must be a purely positive perfection connatural to being itself. Christian philosophers tend to forget that the status of the Second Person (and of the Third too), as pure subsistent Receptivity and Gratitude, is of *absolutely equal worth* and perfection as the self-giving mode of the Father. Hence receptivity, as participated in by the created world, laced with imperfection as it is, must still be a postive perfection and necessary attribute of reality as a whole. The implications for a richer evaluation of the "masculine" and the "feminine" dimensions of human personality are challenging and exciting, but we will leave that development to others more competent. Here once again the special illuminating power of Christian revelation on philosophy itself becomes apparent.

This thematizing of the positive value of receptivity as a primordial dimension of being itself is, I admit, something new in my own thought. I owe it to two principal sources: (1) to the stimulus of Process thinkers like Charles Hartshorne, John Cobb, and Lewis Ford; (2) to the creative (often daring) theological speculation on the Trinity by the Swiss Catholic theologian, Hans Urs von Balthasar, as insightfully gathered together by the Irish theologian, Gerard O'Hanlon, S.J.[18] But gotten clearly into focus, it seems to me an inescapable implication of St. Thomas's own metaphysics of being and phenomenology of the love of friendship.

2) Once it becomes clear that real being tends naturally to spin out a web of relationships with the beings around it – within its horizon of action, we might say – and that these relationships involve interactive relationships of communicating and receiving, it also follows that real beings tend naturally to form some kind of network, or *order*, or *systems* of interaction – may we not say some kind of *community* in the widest sense? These systems or communities appear first as many, but then keep opening out in ever wider interlocking circles. And in virtue of the metaphysics of participation of all finite being in the perfection emanating from a single ultimate, intelligent Source, all lesser systems finally

become integrated into a single all-embracing community of all real being. This latter point is not the focus of my concern here, but only the fact that real being, as intrinsically self-communication and relational through action, tends naturally toward modes of being-together that we can justifiably call the mode of community. To be, it turns out, means *to-be-together*. Being and community are inseparable. The empirical evidence for the extraordinary interconnectedness of all things in our own material and personal universe keeps mounting each day, through the findings of physics, cosmology, biology, ecology, sociology, psychology – and theology (e.g., the notion of the Christian community, the Church, the people of God). Even if I but wiggle my finger here on earth, physicists tell us, some minuscule influence will reach to the furthest stars.

At the level of personal being, where consciousness enters in, the ontological community of beings turns into conscious social community in the full sense, as a natural expression and fulfillment of the self-communicating dynamism of being once it transcends the limitations of matter enough to enter the domain of self-conscious freedom. And at its deepest and most intimate level the conscious bonds of human togetherness turn into *communion*. At the finite human level this is a limited participation in the total, infinitely per-

fect communion within God himself, the
circumincessio (or mutual circulation of life)
which is the inner life of God as triunely personal,
where the unity and communion are total, yet the
distinction of persons remains. Personal being,
therefore, *tends ultimately toward communion* as
its natural fulfillment.

3) We may justifiably take one step further,
therefore, and say that all being tends naturally
toward *self-transcendence*. This is clear on the horizontal level in the tendency toward togetherness,
system, and community. But in finite created
beings this includes a natural dynamism towards
attaining their own goodness to the fullest degree
possible. But, as St. Thomas says, since all finite
goods are good only by participation in the
Infinite Good, every finite being tends, as far as its
nature allows, towards imitating, becoming a likeness of, the Divine Goodness. In personal beings,
endowed with intelligence and will, this universal
dynamism towards the Good turns into an innate
implicit longing for personal union with the
Infinite Good, "the natural desire for the Beatific
Vision," as Aquinas puts it. The whole universe,
then, for him, turns into an immense implicit
aspiration towards the Divine.[19]

II. Application to the Person

Let us now apply this dynamic,
self-communicative notion of being to the person,
specifically the human person. For St. Thomas,
the person is "that which is most perfect in all of
nature."[20] But it is not some special mode of
being, added on from the outside, so to speak. It is
really nothing but the fullness of being itself, existence come into its own, allowed to be fully what
it is by "nature" when not restricted by the limitations proper to the material mode of being. In a
word, when being is allowed to be fully itself as
active *presence*, it *ipso facto* turns into luminous
self-presence and *self-possession*, i.e., self-consciousness in the order of knowledge and self-determination in the order of action. But these are
precisely the essential attributes of person. To *be*
fully, without restriction, therefore, is to be personal.

1. The Meaning of Person

What does it mean, then, precisely, to be *a
person* for St. Thomas? We cannot enter here into
the long and fascinating history of how the
meaning of "person" developed and became
distinct.[21] The distinction developed partly as a
social and legal term in Roman law, where
"person" meant a human being with full legal

rights as a Roman citizen, as distinguished from slaves, who were indeed human beings, but not persons. But the most urgent pressure came from the Christian theologians to explicate more precisely the two central Christian doctrines of God as Triune (one God, with one divine nature possessed equally by the three "owners" or persons), and the Incarnation (God become man in Jesus Christ, so that the human nature of Jesus is not a person on its own but is "owned" by the Second Divine Person, the Son, who now possesses two natures, one divine, possessed from all eternity, the other human, taken on in time). Thus Christ is one Divine Person owning two natures, whereas God in himself is one divine nature owned by three distinct Persons. The distinction between person and nature now had to take on more than a merely social or legal meaning, that is, an ontological one in the order of being itself.

In terms of his central metaphysical doctrine of the distinction between essence (or nature) and the act of existing, St. Thomas was able to give a more elegant and precise explication of the distinction between person and nature than other scholastic thinkers (who were forced to recur to more complicated and to my mind dubious explanations in terms of special modes, negations, etc.). For him, to be a person it is not enough merely to possess a complete individual intellectual nature – which all admitted was an essential requisite, according to the classical definition of Boethius: a person is "an individual substance of a rational nature." To be a person in its own right such a nature would have to possess or "own" its own act of existence (*esse*). Thus the human nature of Christ, though a complete human *nature*, just like ours, was not a human *person*, because it was owned by a Divine Person (the Son or Word of God), in what is technically called the Hypostatic (i.e., personal) Union of God and man. Hence it is the nature's own proportionate act of existence, actualizing it as an existent, which formally constitutes that nature a person. The person is the concrete whole resulting from this union, expressed by the term "I." Ordinary language indicates quite clearly the distinction by two distinct questions: "*who* am I?" (person) and "*what* am I?" (nature).

Thus for St. Thomas the person could be defined as "an intellectual nature possessing its own act of existence, so that it can be the self-conscious, responsible source of its own actions." In a word, in perhaps the briefest – and still one of the best – descriptions of person ever given, a person is a being that is *dominus sui*, that is, master of itself, or *self-possessing* (in the order of knowledge by self-consciousness; in the order of will and action by self-determination or free will).[22]

The above definition – "an intellectual nature possessing its own act of existence" – is indeed, as far as it goes, one accurate expression of St. Thomas's thought. But it has one shortcoming: it does not do justice to the full metaphysical richness and originality of his doctrine of existence as central act and core of all perfection in a real being. For according to the now generally accepted interpretation of "Thomistic existentialism" (since Gilson, De Finance, etc.), the act of existence is not merely the actualization from without, so to speak, of the perfections somehow already present potentially in the essence in its own right; it is rather the whole positive core and content of *all* the perfection that is actualized in the essence. Thus the essence (in a finite created being) is really only a particular limiting mode of existence, which constricts the all-embracing fullness of perfection that is existence itself down to some determinate, limited participation.

Thus any finite being is really a limited act of existence, existing now as a new whole distinct from all other real beings. Once this whole has been constituted, one can then speak of the existing essence or nature as the subject of existing or as possessing its own act of existence, as long as this does not obscure the fact that all the positive perfection of this subject flows into it from its act of existence.

Thus a perhaps more adequate definition of person for St. Thomas might be this: a *person* is "an actual existent [i.e., with its own act of existence], distinct from all others, possessing an intellectual nature, so that it can be the self-conscious, responsible source of its own actions." A *human* person would be an actual existent, distinct from all others, possessing only a human intellectual nature (i.e., as embodied spirit). This is actually very close, almost a translation, of one of Thomas's favorite definitions of person, *subsistens distinctum in natura rationali* (a distinct subsistent in a rational nature). Here he clearly goes beyond the classical formula of Boethius, "an individual substance of a rational nature," since "subsistent" for Thomas means an actual existent, existing in itself (in the mode of substance) with its own act of existence.[23]

The advantage of working from this second definition, where the emphasis is on the act of existence as central rather than the nature, is this: if all the perfection of being a person comes to it from its act of existence, proportioned of course to its nature, then we can transfer all the attributes characteristic of existence itself over into the person as such, where they will be found at enhanced degrees of intensity. This is what we intend to do in the second half of this lecture.

It should be noted that neither of the two definitions of person for St. Thomas that I have given above occurs in its complete form in any one text of St. Thomas, so far as I know. I have deliberately combined two perspectives, the metaphysical and the anthropological. The first part of each definition, e.g., "a distinct existent possessing an intellectual nature," expresses the metaphysical foundation-structure of the person; the second part, e.g., "the self-conscious, responsible source of its own actions," or "self-mastery," expresses the manifestation of this ontological constitution in the order of activity, and is found principally in the various treatises on human nature and ethics. Both are in St. Thomas in equivalent words; I have combined them together in order to show the significant overlap between his analysis and that of most later philosophers, which is ordinarily less concerned with the metaphysical roots and more with the phenomenological manifestations of personhood in human beings. Thus there is a wide general consensus, I think, among most modern and contemporary philosophers who take the person seriously, that to be a person signifies a being that is the self-conscious, responsible source of its own actions. As Amelie Rorty, a well-known analytic philosopher who has written a great deal about the person, sums it up: "the idea of a person is the idea of a unified center of choice and action, the unit of legal, moral, and theological responsibility." St. Thomas would agree, but prefers to penetrate more deeply into the metaphysical roots of this self-mastery. A useful synthesis of his two perspectives, without using his technical metaphysical terms, may be found in the excellent article on "Person" by Max Müller and Alois Halder in the theological encyclopedia edited by Karl Rahner and his team of collaborators, *Sacramentum Mundi*:

> Person does not mean "essence" or "nature" but the actual unique reality of a spiritual being, an undivided whole existing independently and not interchangeable with any other ... the reality of a being which belongs to itself and is therefore its own end in itself. It is the concrete form taken by the freedom of a spiritual being, on which is based its inviolable dignity.[24]

A highly condensed but still accurate definition of the person for St. Thomas has been worked out by the always insightful Thomistic metaphysician, Umberto degl'Innocenti, O.P., in his fine technical study, *Il Problema della persona nel pensiero di San Tommaso*: "A person is an autonomous existent of an intellectual nature" (or *ens autonomum intellectuale*).[25] The idea should be clear.

The notion of person, however, is an analogous one, ranging over several different levels of being, determined by the kind of intellectual nature which the person possesses as its own. The three that we know of – there may in principle be more – are the human, the angelic (i.e., purely spiritual but created, finite beings), and the divine. Since our focus is on the human person, and since the kind of nature possessed by a human person, that of an embodied spirit, significantly modifies how the basic ontological properties of the person are actualized and expressed in the real order, I think it wise to preface this new section with a brief summary of the ontological structure of human nature as such, as understood by St. Thomas.

2. Structure of Human Nature

A *human* person is a personal being possessing its intellectual nature as joined in a natural unity with a material body. Aristotle defined this unity called "man" as "a rational animal." St. Thomas too accepts this and uses it often. But a profounder and more exact description in terms of St. Thomas's own total vision of man would be *embodied spirit*.[26] The two perspectives are different, though by no means contradictory. "Rational animal" signifies man's place as the highest of the animals, starting from this material world of our experience as its frame of reference and moving *upwards*. "Embodied spirit" signifies man's place in a total vision of the hierarchy of being, looking *downwards* from God as Infinite Spirit, through the various levels of finite pure spirits (angels), then down through man as embodied spirit, all the way to the lowest levels of purely material being. In this perspective man takes his place as the lowest of the spirits, coming into existence in a body, without innate ideas (such as the angels have by a finite participation in the creative ideas of God); its destiny is to make its way back to God by a journey through the material world, coming to know and work with the latter through the mediation of its multi-sensed body.

By coming to understand the meaning of the material world and of its own self in it, and following out the implications as far as they lead, a human being can finally rise to an indirect, analogous knowledge and direct love of the Transcendent Spiritual Source of itself and its cosmos, "led by the hand by material things," as St. Thomas graphically puts it.[27] This journey is a distinctively human one, quite different from that of the angels. "Embodied spirit" expresses better than "rational animal" this vaster perspective, wherein man appears in his deepest level of being as spirit, but a spirit that needs the body as a natural complement and mediating instrument to fulfill his destiny as a traveller to God through the material cosmos – *homo viator*, man the traveller, as the medievals loved to call him.

The actual philosophical process of discovery of the nature of the human being as carried out by St. Thomas follows at first the Aristotelian path of moving from the manifest characteristic activities of the creature we recognize as human, as like us, to the hidden abiding center and source of these actions, what we call its nature. But once it reaches the deepest levels of this human nature as spirit and as related to God, its Ultimate Source and Final End, Thomas goes far beyond Aristotle – who gets stuck in philosophical impasses and incoherencies at this point – to construct his own original Christian synthesis, both philosophical and theological. Since it is not our purpose in this lecture to focus on the philosophical analysis of human nature as such, which has already been ably developed in well-known treatises of Thomistic philosophical anthropology, but rather on the human being as person, it will be enough for our purposes to recapitulate briefly the main themes of such an analysis, under the following headings:

1) An individual human nature is a natural unity of body and intellectual soul, each complementary to the other. Since this soul, the unifying center of all vital activities in the body, also performs purely spiritual acts of intelligence and will transcending any bodily organs, the soul must possess its own spiritual act of existence, transcending the body, which it then "lends" to the body, so to speak, drawing the latter up into itself to participate in this higher mode of being as the necessary instrument for the soul's own journey of self-realization through the material cosmos as embodied spirit, the lowest of the spirits. The human soul and body thus form a single unified existing nature. But because the soul possesses its own spiritual act of existence in its own right as spirit, it can retain this existence even when separated from its bodily partner at death, though it always retains its intrinsic orientation towards this body and will rejoin the latter again in the final resurrection of the body. Thus the human soul is not just the "form of the body," as it seems to be for Aristotle, but a form *plus*, a spirit *and* a form, a spirit which does indeed operate as a form within the body but also transcends it with higher operations of its own – a synthesis which is Thomas's own, going beyond both St. Augustine and Aristotle.

2) The human will, as the soul's faculty of action flowing from its intellectual nature, is also a spiritual faculty like the intellect. And precisely because, as spirit, it is necessarily oriented towards nothing less than the Infinite Good as its only adequate fulfillment, no finite good can command its adherence by necessity, and it remains free to choose its own path toward the Infinite among all finite goods, even to turn away on the conscious level from its own authentic Good towards other apparent goods through self-induced or culpable "ignorance."

3) The human intellect, as capacity for being (*capax entis*), is naturally ordered, as to its adequate object, to the whole of being as intelligible. Hence it can ultimately be satisfied only by knowing directly the infinite source and fullness of all being, namely, God (*capax entis, ergo capax Dei*). So too the human will, the faculty tending towards being as good, is naturally ordered to the whole order of the good without restriction. Hence it too cannot ultimately be satisfied by anything less than loving union with God as the infinite fullness of all goodness. Thus we are magnetized, so to speak, by our very nature toward the Infinite Good, which draws us in our very depths, at first spontaneously below the level of consciousness and freedom, but then slowly emerging into consciousness as we grow older – if we allow

it – by the accumulation of experience and reflection upon it.

This innate, unrestricted drive of the human spirit (and of all finite spirits, embodied or not) toward the Infinite Good is the great hidden dynamo that energizes our whole lives, driving us on to ever new levels of growth and development, and refusing to let us be ultimately contented with any merely finite, especially material, goods, whether we understand consciously what is going on within us or not, whether we can explicitly identify our final goal or not. As Augustine put it so well in his classic saying, "Our hearts are restless, O Lord, till they rest in You." This radical dynamism rooted in our spiritual nature might be called the *dynamic a priori* of the human spirit as such, and thus of every human person.[28]

4) Thus the human being, because of its dual nature as embodied spirit, spirit wedded to matter, becomes indeed a "microcosm," as the ancients put it: i.e., a synthesis of the whole universe. By his body he sinks his roots deep into the material cosmos, which provides the initial input for his thought and action and the theater (in this life) for his journey toward self-realization. But by his spiritual soul he rises above the dispersion of space and time to live in the spiritual horizon of supra-material meanings and values and to set his sights on the Infinite and the

Eternal. Thus to be a human being, as St. Thomas phrases it, echoing Plotinus and several of the early Christian writers, is "to live on the edge, on the frontier of matter and spirit, time and eternity," to be an "amphibian," as the Greek Fathers put it, able at will to direct himself in either direction, down toward matter or up toward spirit. His destiny is thus to journey through matter toward a fulfillment beyond matter.[29]

5) This human journey must be a *social* one, together with, in community with, other human beings. Human beings are intrinsically social in nature, not only because of mutual dependence and complementarity, but also because it is natural for us "to take delight in living together with other human beings," as St. Thomas puts it. This will be developed more in our second characteristic of personal living, and was already clearly recognized by St. Thomas.

This journey must also be an *historical* one, unlike that of any of the subhuman species on our earth (who also become part of a very slow overall evolving history of the earth and indeed the whole material universe, but not one fueled by the creative freedom of its individual participants). The emphasis on the radical "historicity" or historical character of the human race as it unfolds its potentialities creatively through time is indeed a new theme very dear to modern and especially contemporary thought,[30] one which St. Thomas himself did not develop explicitly because it was not yet in focus in his time, more interested in discovering the permanent laws of nature. Yet I think he would have been quite open to such a perspective, as long as it did not overthrow the abiding identity of human nature through history. For, unlike animals, the unrestricted range of man's intellectual power and interests, matched by the corresponding freedom of his will, give him an inexhaustible creativity to express himself in constantly new – and not always predictable – cultural forms, instruments, and ways of interacting with nature – give him, in a word, the ability freely to *make his own history* as he journeys down through time. And in so doing the human actor molds not only the world around him but his own self as he goes. Thus in our contemporary world the turn to historicity has invaded every discipline, and no attempt at explanation in any field, whether science, philosophy, theology, art, society, etc., can be accepted as adequate unless it includes the historical or genetic aspect of the thing to be explained. This is as it should be, and marks a definite advance in our human understanding of the real world we live in.

There is a danger, however, in this enthusiasm for historicity that St. Thomas would have warned against. Some proponents have opposed

historicity and nature in human culture so sharply
that the first simply cancels out the second; thus
they define a human being as one whose *only nature* is to have no nature but to create it freely in
history as he goes. There is no need to go this far
(in fact the coherence of the statement crumbles
under closer inspection) in order to do justice to
the authentic historicity of the human. The
Thomistic understanding of human nature as
embodied spirit, or even rational animal, does not
imply a static structure, rigidly determined in all
its details, but rather a dynamic center of free,
self-conscious action on two levels (material and
spiritual), whose outside limits of development are
set a priori only as those of a spirit united to a
material body. This leaves an immense open field
for unpredictable development within these broad
parameters, telling us nothing a priori about what
the bodily instrument of the soul is going to look
like at a given time or for how long, or what kind
of environment, inner and outer, this free creative
spirit will produce through its instruments. None
of the most varied forms of culture or technology
produced in the long course of human history
gives us the slightest evidence for believing we are
dealing with anything else than an embodied
spirit. In fact, this immense variety is exactly what
we would expect from a being whose *nature* it is to
possess creative freedom. The dynamic Thomistic

notion of both nature and substance, as ordered towards self-expression through action, outlined in the first part of this lecture, is, however, obviously necessary to integrate adequately the historical dimension into its understanding of human nature.

If we now put together all the above elements in our analysis of human nature, with its classical Thomistic and contemporary components, we may expand our previous description of human nature as follows: a human being is by nature a finite embodied spirit, in search of the Infinite, in social solidarity with its fellow human beings, on an historical journey through this material cosmos towards its final trans-worldly goal.

Now that we have explicated the Thomistic conceptions of both person and human nature, we are in a position to proceed directly to the second part of our lecture: namely, the main ways in which the human person manifests or gives expression in actual living to the inner structure of its personalized being. All these ways, as we have said, will be rooted in the act of existence which constitutes it as person, adjusted appropriately to fit the human nature which possesses it as its own. Although St. Thomas himself does not give us any one systematic exposition of these characteristics gathered together in one place as I am doing here, all the elements appear in some equivalent way at appropriate places in his treatment of the human person, so that my own selective and creative reconstruction is, I believe, fundamentally faithful to his thought, though it will go beyond what he has said explicitly in its integration of certain contemporary insights. I did promise at the beginning that this would be a "creative completion" of St. Thomas's own work. I shall divide these characteristics of personal living into three basic ones: Personal Being as Self-possessing; Personal Being as Self-communicative and Relational; and Personal Being as Self-transcending. From now on when I speak of "the person," I shall be referring to the person as realized in a human nature.

3. The Person as Self-possessing

In the first part of our study on St. Thomas's understanding of what it means to be, we called attention to the *dyadic* structure of all real being: to be is to be substance-in-relation. Thus every real being exists first as present *in itself*, standing on its own as a unity-identity-whole in the midst of the community of existents, i.e., not as a part of any other being (though it can certainly be related to others); then it tends naturally to pour over into active *self-communication* with other real beings, generating relations, community, etc. We stressed especially this second aspect, as having been too long overlooked in St. Thomas for a static view of substance. But we also warned that this self-communicating, relational aspect of being, important though it is, must not be cut off from its ontological root in the substantial or in-itself aspect of being, lest the whole fabric of reality collapse into the emptiness of purely relational being, as the Buddhists argue.

So too with the human person. This presence in itself proper to every real being, when raised to the level of spiritual being as transcending the dispersal of matter, manifests itself on the conscious level as a luminous self-presence which we call *self-consciousness*, awareness of oneself both as present and as source of one's actions. This is what I have chosen to call *self-possession*, following St. Thomas's wonderfully terse description of the human being as *dominus sui* (master of itself). This self-possession finds expression in two main ways: (1) in the order of knowledge, through *self-consciousness* or self-awareness, which enables the person to meaningfully say "I"; (2) in the order of action, through *self-determination* or freedom of the will, which enables the person to say, "I am responsible for this action." Let us examine each one in turn.

(1) *Self-possession as self-consciousness*. This self-presence enables a personal being to be aware of itself, not as object, distinct from or "out in front of itself," so to speak (*ob-jectum* = lying

before one), but as *subject*, immediately present to itself from within, as source of its own actions such that it can meaningfully say "I" – an expression with its own unique logic indicating that the speaker knows himself as speaker in the same act that he knows whatever else he is speaking about. To be able meaningfully to say "I" is the unique prerogative of personal being. That is why animals are not persons. Although they are aware through their senses of the outside world, they are locked into an extraverted focusing on the objects of their senses and cannot make that "full return of the soul to itself," as St. Thomas puts it, which would enable them to be *self-present* as well as present to others, in a word, to be self-conscious.[31] This identity or coincidence of knower and known in the one act when we say "I" is one of the evidences brought forward by St. Thomas, together with many later thinkers, for asserting that the inner principle of such action must be a spiritual soul.[32] For one essential note of material being is dispersal over extended space, which does not allow any part of a material being to coincide or be identical with any other part, or with any part of itself. To coincide fully with oneself, so that both the subject and the object of the same act are identical, as in the act of self-awareness, reveals that the subject of such an activity must transcend the self-dispersal, or "spread-outness," of the material mode of being as such, pointing to a more intense and concentrated level of self-presence that we call "spiritual being."

In the higher ranges of personal being, such as in God and the angels, this self-presence is immediate, totally transparent, and complete. Having no bodies they have no submerged unconscious dimension and no slow education process spread over time. Not so with the human person, as embodied spirit. Our intellectual consciousness starts off not yet in act, but potential, in the dark, so to speak. It must be activated from without, first by a movement outward toward the material world, then, actuated by the stimulus of incoming sense knowledge and intellectual response to it, it returns back to its spiritual source within and lights up in conscious self-presence. Like the Sleeping Beauty, we must first be touched by another before we can wake up to ourselves. This process of awakening from latent to explicit self-consciousness is one that unfolds slowly, spread out over several years of time. And it seems that the explicit awakening to self-awareness as an "I," as a self, can only be done by another human person, reaching out to us with love and treating us as a person, calling us into an I-Thou relation. So we must first go out to the external world, in particular to other persons, and then return to our center, newly awakened to recognize ourselves explic-

itly as persons. The relation to others comes first,
then the awakening to ourselves as persons. This
early process has been beautifully described by
John Macmurray (among others) in his book,
Persons in Relation.[33]

The process then continues on, through
adolescence, where the young person is trying to
distinguish itself from its parents and relate to its
peers, especially of the opposite sex, through
young adulthood and beyond, where gradually,
through experience, reflection on it, and taking
responsibility for our actions, we come to take
fuller conscious possession of our own unique personality, to discover just "who I am" as a unique
distinctive person among other persons in the
world. The process actually continues all through
one's life – ideally – as new facets of the self that
were formerly in shadow slowly emerge into the
light. There are still quite a few surprises left even
after one has reached 70, as I can testify from
experience.

It does not seem, however, that the process
of self-possession through self-knowledge can ever
reach a final stage of completeness and total clar-
ity for a human person at any time throughout his
life, at least this present chapter of it. The human
self remains always a "known-unknown," a mysterious abyss, in which more remains unknown
than known, like the tip of an iceberg emerging

above water. The vast depths of our unconscious, both individual and collective, remain either unknown or only partially and indirectly accessible to consciousness. But most of all there is the natural depth of the self, stemming from the fact that as spiritual intellect and will we are naturally open to, and have a natural drive towards the whole of being as both intelligible and good. Since this includes implicitly Infinite Being itself, there is a kind of infinite or inexhaustible depth in our spirit, due to its openness to the Infinite, which cannot be plumbed by our explicit consciousness short of the direct vision of God himself, when we shall see ourselves totally as God sees us, i.e., as we really are. As the German mystical poet, Angelus Silesius, puts it, "The abyss in man cries out to the abyss in God. Tell me, which is deeper?" Thus our self-awareness is a partial zone of light within us, ever in fluid expansion or recession, surrounded by a penumbra of shadow shading off into an (at present) impenetrable darkness. St. Augustine once said that the whole aim of his philosophy was "to know myself and to know Thee, O God." Actually the two focuses of knowledge advance together, in an alternating spiral of reciprocal illumination until the final vision. As that ninth-century genius, John Scotus Eriugena, put it brilliantly: "God and man are paradigms of each other." Both are ultimately ineffable, and this both because of their subjectivity and their inexhaustible depth.[34]

St. Thomas himself was aware in his own way of this unsoundable depth of the human person when he pointed out that, although we do know immediately and self-evidently that we exist and are the *source* of our own actions, the same is not true of the nature or *essence* of the human soul, what *kind* of being it is. This requires a long and difficult investigation, and many can disagree on the results. Man is a traveller, therefore, in his self-knowledge as well as in all the other aspects of his being.[35]

(2) *Self-possession through self-determination*. The second mode of self-possession proper to personal being is in the order of action, achieved through self-determination, i.e., mastery over our own actions by freedom of the will. This enables the person to say, "I am *responsible* for this action." Moral responsibility flows immediately from this self-possession through freedom. The "I" of the person is where the buck stops in assigning responsibility for an act as moral. "*I* did it," "*I* am sorry," "*I* deserve praise or blame," not some subconscious impulse, some environmental or social pressure, something external to me – higher or lower, good or evil – taking me over ("Some god must have blinded me," as the Greek heroes in Homer's epics used to say when some

disordered action of theirs led to disaster.) A personal being is therefore one that is in charge of its own life, a *self-governing* being.

It is worth pausing for a moment to reflect on the profound implications of this distinguishing note of the person as self-governing, as master of its own actions. Herein lies the true dignity of every personal being, and hence of ourselves as human persons. Animals are not persons both because they are not consciously aware of themselves and because, as a consequence, they cannot be masters of their own action, cannot be self-determining through free will, in charge of their own lives. Their actions are governed for the most part by built-in, inherited, or unconsciously acquired instincts more proper to the species as a whole than to the individual as such. Hence, though animals are the ontological source of their actions, they are not morally responsible for them. (St. Thomas does concede, however, that animals, especially the higher ones, do possess a certain spontaneity of choice that is a limited participation in the higher self-conscious freedom that characterizes human persons.) Animals, in a word, are not self-possessing beings, either in knowledge or in action; they are not masters of themselves as we are by our personal mode of being.

St. Thomas locates the true moral dignity of
man, that by which man is an image of God in his
moral life, precisely in this capacity to be *self-
governing*, to freely and deliberately guide himself
toward God as his final goal, using all the wisdom
available to him, whether natural or supernatural,
in other words, to exercise *providence* over his
own life. It is indeed true that man is called to
exercise his self-government according to the natural law that is "imprinted in his heart" as part of
his nature, which itself is a participation in the
divine law (God's normative idea for man). Still, it
is not in mere blind obedience to this inner law
that the moral life becomes an image of God; for
God does not act in obedience to any law. It is
precisely in that man exercises *intelligent free self-*
government, or *providence* over his own life
according to this law that he is acting as an image
of God. For God in his infinitely wise and all-
comprehensive providence governs the whole of
creation and guides it to its final end. Now a
human person cannot take responsibility for governing the whole of creation (unless he has forgotten that he is human, has lost his self-possession).
But he can imitate God in his own limited human
way by responsibly exercising providence over his
own little corner of the universe that is under his
control, i.e., his own life in its social context
(including those he is responsible for), guiding it

toward its final end as best he can, with a view toward harmonizing it with the good of the whole universe, just as God does. His limited providence is an image of the all-comprehensive Providence of God.[36]

Thomists have always been proud of this distinctive aspect of St. Thomas's ethics, namely, that his morality is not primarily a morality of *obedience* to law, in the sense of obedience to particular precepts imposed explicitly from without – as is the case with the ethics of William of Ockham and the Nominalist tradition – but a morality of the free self-governing person, responsibly guiding itself towards God as final goal, in accordance with the flexible inner law – called the natural law – imprinted in the person's very nature by God, but speaking now to the person through its own inner light of wisdom, such as it in fact is. It is as though the basic moral law were: "*Be* fully what you in fact *are*," or better: "*Become* fully what you already *are*, in the deepest, most authentic longing of your nature." Thus the fully mature moral person does good and avoids evil, not primarily because he will be rewarded or punished according to some law imposed from without, but precisely because he sees it as something *good* to do (or avoid), in creative harmony with his own nature and the whole order of the good as willed by God, in a word, as another step towards his final goal – which in fact, recognized or not – will be union with God.[37]

In accordance with this strong emphasis on responsible self-government as the core of the moral life, St. Thomas does not hesitate to draw conclusions on the meaning and practice of obedience to a human superior that have seemed quite daring to some, as I have repeatedly found in lecturing to contemporary Catholic audiences. For example, in speaking of the obedience one owes to a legitimate superior, such as a bishop, Thomas makes the following significant statement:

> It is not the place of the subject to pass judgment on the command in itself in its own wisdom and goodness, but it is his responsibility to pass judgment on his own fulfilling of the command here and now. For every person is bound to examine his own actions according to the knowledge which he himself has from God, whether natural or acquired, or infused from above; for every man is obliged to act according to reason [i.e., in context according to his or her own *personal participation* in reason].[38]

In a word, responsible obedience, which alone is worthy of the moral dignity of the human person, requires that I myself freely and responsibly judge whether it is here and now *good* for me to obey, a judgment that cannot be abdicated to anyone else, even to the Pope himself, or an angel. What a ringing affirmation of the responsible freedom of the mature moral person under God!

I recall some years ago (about 15 or 20, I think) reading this text to a group of nuns during a retreat or day of recollection, but not telling them where it came from. Then I asked them what they thought of it, and the reply was, "That's pretty far-out; that's not the traditional Catholic position." When I replied that this was from St. Thomas Aquinas, they answered, "They certainly didn't teach us that in the novitiate." I tried the same thing only about ten years ago at a talk given to the Newman Club at New York University, and an obviously very conservative Catholic man burst out, "We can't accept that; if the Pope tells you to do something, you do it. He's the highest authority for a Catholic." When I told him this was from St. Thomas himself, he replied without a moment's hesitation, "Well, he'll have to go." Yet this is not at all some far-out, eccentric position of St. Thomas, singing out of chorus. It *is* the authentic Christian moral tradition, that appears strange only to those who have lost touch with it. Has not St. Thomas, after all, been declared by several Popes to be the "common doctor" of the Church (*doctor communis*)?

Karol Wojtyla (our present Pope) in his philosophical writings has carried a significant step further the analysis of self-determination we have presented above, drawn directly from St. Thomas, and in fact gently reproves St. Thomas for not doing so himself.[39] Although it is true that Aquinas did not develop this aspect explicitly, I think it is perfectly in accord with the inner logic of his own thought and that he would have been quite pleased with this "creative completion" of it in the line of a phenomenology of the moral life. This new aspect is the insight that in exercising our freedom of choice we are not only freely determining our particular actions – as St. Thomas develops in detail – but we are also determining *our own very selves* as persons, our personal character, in a word, "*who* we are." For the particular action, if done consciously and responsibly, is inescapably *my* action, and thus commits *me*, the whole person behind the act, more or less profoundly according to the seriousness of the act and the degree of my conscious commitment to it, to the value embedded in the act, so that it leaves a more or less profound trace in me beyond the immediate conscious awareness of the act and its apparent consequences. And in the very experience of such a self-determining act one is aware, at least implicitly, of this double aspect, that is, both the objective worth of the act in itself and its effect upon the chooser. Thus in every free, responsible act, as Sr. Mary Clark puts it so aptly, "one determines oneself not only to act but also to be."[40] By my actions, therefore, especially the repeated ones, I gradually construct an abiding moral portrait of myself, like an artist's self-portrait, proclaiming implicitly, "This is the kind of person I am."

We can indeed repudiate later with regret certain actions, but they cannot help but leave some trace in us outlasting the particular event. We are not like a computer, in which an entry or program held in storage can be simply wiped out at will without leaving a trace. Every consciously chosen action, then, helps to mold and construct our own very selves, "who we are" in the moral order, at a deeper level than the action taken by itself. In a word, our personal identity in the existential order of action is inseparable from our *story* as a whole, a story we must interpret and integrate to make fully meaningful, but cannot repudiate. That is why, as Charles Taylor points out so insightfully in his book, *The Sources of the Self*, a significant part of our self-identity, part of our answer to the question, "Who are you?" must include our moral stance, or, as he puts it, "What do you stand for?" (i.e., what values, etc.).[41]

The above as analysis of the self-determination of our free actions as also *self*-determination adds a deeper – and considerably mere sobering – dimension to the notion of self-possession as a basic characteristic of the life of the human person. It adds a distinctive overtone of seriousness and personal involvement to the whole moral enterprise that I think St. Thomas himself would have welcomed and seen, in fact, as necessarily implied in his own teaching that nothing less than the whole person is the ultimate responsible source of every free action, as well as in his highly developed analysis of the role of virtue in the moral life. But Wojtyla's complaint against St. Thomas is that he develops his analysis of the free act exclusively along the line of the outward-oriented intentionality of the act towards its object, leaving out of consideration the inward-oriented effect of *self*-determination or *self*-making that goes hand in hand with the former. In a word, the intentionality of the act is object-oriented; the concomitant intentionality of self-determination is subject-oriented. The two aspects are inseparable but distinct. I think the Cardinal is right in pointing out this lacuna in St. Thomas. But I also think it is very easy to fill it by a creative following out of the inner dynamism of Aquinas's own thought.

In concluding this section on *self-possession* as the first characteristic of authentic personal living, I would like to highlight once again its importance and how this is endangered by many contemporary analyses of the person. Self-possession is the manifestation on the level of conscious experience of one of the two complementary poles of the underlying ontological structure of the person, namely, its in-itselfness or substantiality, by which it stands out as a distinct, autonomous, self-governing moral subject in the community of other persons and of all beings. It is here that the unique inner depth of privacy and interiority of the personal self resides, irreducible to any of its outward-facing relations, and without which the latter lose their own grounding in being. For unless one has some distinct self to give or share, and some conscious possession of it as one's own, how could one "give oneself to another" in friendship and love, as the phenomenological analyses describe so eloquently? Similarly, could there really be "another self" to receive our gift?

This *conscious* self-awareness of our own uniqueness and interior depth is also important as a support for our sense of self-worth and dignity, as a protection against the pathological feeling of loss of self and fusing into others, so that we become totally passive to what others expect and wish of us, and finally lose any real sense of "who we are." John Crosby has given us a salutary warning against this "heteropathic" dissolving of ourselves into our relations with others, so that we became a mere doormat or mirror for them, losing our own sense of uniqueness and dignity in the process. There can be an unhealthy as well as a healthy meaning of the "loss of self" that the great spiritual traditions invite us to as the highest perfection. It is well not to forget this in our enthusiasm for "self-emptying" ("kenotic") spiritualities and methods of meditation.[42]

The failure to do justice to the substantiality pole of the person seems to me the most serious lacuna in most contemporary phenomenologies of the person as relational and interpersonal. One group, the more moderate, holds that the person does have an in-itself dimension, but that it is *constituted*, brought into existence as a person, by one's relations to others; for the child this means by the initiative of other already constituted persons reaching out to it and calling it to personhood.

Metaphysically this will not work. We cannot literally bring into being another person that was not there before simply by relating to the thing that is there with attentive love. Try doing this with a rock, a tree, or a rattlesnake! The being to which we relate must already be of the type that *can* respond to such an invitation by intrinsic powers already within it. The better way of providing adequate metaphysical grounding for their fine descriptive analyses is to analyze the appearance in the child of conscious personal responses as the awakening into actuality of a potentiality or capacity already latent there in the child's own being (as intellectual nature) and needing only the appropriate outside stimulus to emerge into actual consciousness. To be a *human* person is to be on a journey from potential self-possession to actual. It is quite true that in the order of time and actuality consciously operative self-possession as a person appears only subsequently to initiatives taken from without, i.e., to incoming relations. But it does not follow at all that these incoming relations actually *constitute* in being the very nature of that to which they relate. The person is awakened to actual exercise of its personhood by the initiatives of others, but is not constituted in being as person by them.

The second and more radical group, influenced by their rejection of one or more of modern philosophy's misconceptions of classical substance, attempt to reduce the human person to nothing more than *the set of its relations* to others. But this not only suffers from the fatal metaphysical flaw of evacuating all persons – in fact all this-worldly being – of any "own-being," so that they disappear into the Buddhist *sunyatta*, or emptiness, as we have pointed out earlier. It also evacuates the whole inner depth dimension of privacy, interiority, irreducible uniqueness and *self*-possession of the person, so that the latter turns into a totally extraverted presence *to* ..., with no interiority or genuine self-presence. While some do this reduction only because of their aversion to substance, like Heidegger, others, like the Deconstructionists and Postmodernists, rejoice in this evacuation of interiority, proclaiming "we have declared war on interiority." What a paradoxical – and infinitely sad – outcome of this Nietzsche-inspired line of modern philosophy, that it should end up by repudiating the very creative subject that thought it up in the first place, that we should witness the final suicide of the subject itself, of the Superman!

Before letting go of this section on self-possession through *self-determination*, we must sound again the warning we noted earlier with respect to self-possession through self-consciousness. Our self-determination, our self-mastery in the order of action through free choice, can never become complete and perfect at any time during our present lives on this earth. There are many influences at work on us that lie outside the limited spotlight of our conscious awareness, coming unnoticed from our family inheritance, our cul-

ture, our environment, and especially our unconscious, and exercising pressures we cannot always
fully control, especially since we are not even
aware of them. There is also the lack of full
integration of the various drives and appetites
within us, the "war within us," as St. Paul
describes it so vividly, "I cannot even understand
my own actions. . . . What happens is that I do, not
the good I will to do, but the evil I do not
intend. . . . My inner self agrees with the law of
God, but I see in my body's members another law
at war with the law of my mind; this makes me the
prisoner of the law of sin in my members. What a
wretched man am I! Who can free me from this
body under the power of death?" (Rom 7:15-25).
In a word, we are not fully masters in our own
house.

Yet if we are not psychologically retarded in
some radical way, we can gradually learn to exercise enough self-mastery over the significant
choices in our lives to be called moral persons,
however imperfectly and incompletely. Self-
possession in the order of action, then, like self-
possession in the order of knowledge, is itself a
journey, an ongoing project never quite completed
in this life, but one that can be approximated
more and more by the discipline of responsible
self-reflection and the development of virtue.
What a difference there is in the self-possession,

the self-awareness and self-mastery of the various
human persons we know! Yet they are all persons,
more or less fully actualized in their potentialities,
more or less fully *themselves*. I cannot think of a
better way to conclude this whole section of our
analysis than by making our own Karl Rahner's
own summary of what it means to be a human
person:

> Being a person, then, means the self-
> possession of a subject as such in a con-
> scious and free relationship to the totality
> of itself. This relationship is the condition
> of possibility and antecedent horizon for
> the fact that in his individual empirical
> experiences and in his individual sciences
> man has to do with himself as one and as a
> whole. Because man's having responsibility
> for the totality of himself is the condition
> for his empirical experience of self, it can-
> not be derived completely from this experi-
> ence and its objectivities. Even when man
> would want to shift all responsibility for
> himself away from himself as someone
> totally determined from without, and thus
> would want to explain himself away, *he* is
> the one who does this and does it knowingly
> and willingly. *He* is the one who
> encompasses the sum of all the possible
> elements of such an explanation, and thus

he is the one who shows himself to be something other than the subsequent product of such individual elements. . . .

Man's actual presence to himself in which he confronts his own system with all its present and future possibilities, and hence confronts himself in his entirety, and places himself in question and thus transcends it, this self-presence cannot be explained after the model of a self-regulating multiple system . . . it cannot explain how man confronts himself in his totality and places himself in question, and how he reflects upon the question of raising questions. . . . To say that man is person and subject, therefore, means first of all that man is someone who cannot be derived, who cannot be produced completely from other elements at our disposal. He is that being who is responsible for himself. When he explains himself, analyzes himself, reduces himself back to the plurality of his origins, he is affirming himself as the subject who is doing this, and in so doing he experiences himself as necessarily prior to and more original than this plurality.[43]

4. The Person as Self-communicative and Relational

We have just seen the "introverted" side of the person, its abiding presence in the world as presence in itself and to itself, as self-possessing through self-consciousness and self-determination. Now we must turn to its "extraverted" side, its relational aspect, by which it is actively present to others, both by its self-communication and its receptivity. All being, as we said earlier, is caught up in this unending dialectic of the within and the without, the in-itself and the toward-others, the inward-facing act of existential presence in itself, and the outward-facing act of self-expression and self-manifestation to others, by which it enters into a web of relationships with them. So too the whole life of a personal being, even more intensely, revolves around this basic polarity of presence to self and presence to others. A person, like every other real being, is a living synthesis of substantiality and relationality, and the relational side is equally important as the substantial side, because it is only through the former that the self as substance can actualize its potentiality and fulfill its destiny.

This is especially true of the human person. For human consciousness does not start off in full, luminous self-presence, like the angels. It begins rather in a kind of darkness, somewhat like a dark theatre, in a state of potency toward knowing all things, in act toward none. To actualize itself, make it luminously present to itself in act, it must first open itself to the world of others, be waked up by their action on it and its own active response, as the Sleeping Beauty in the symbolic fairy tale must be waked up by a kiss from without. Only then, through the mediation of the other, can it return to itself, to discover itself as self-conscious "I," as this unique human person. I distinguish myself from the subhuman world around me by responding to it, by interacting with it and discovering that it is *not* like me, neither articulate, nor self-conscious, nor free, as I am. I discover positively what and who I am by engaging actively – and receptively – in interpersonal relations with other human beings like me who treat me as a "Thou" in an interpersonal social matrix of "I-Thou-We." The pervasive role of the human community and human culture as indispensable in the coming to self-possession should be given due place here, and could be developed at length. But I am sure you are sufficiently acquainted with this aspect of human personality not to need detailed spelling out by me.

St. Thomas was quite explicit in stressing the social nature of human beings in general, how they need each other in an ordered social matrix to develop properly and satisfy their needs on all levels. He even has a lovely phrase about the spontaneous natural joy there is in human community when he remarks, "It is natural for human beings to take delight in living together (*delectabiliter vivere in communi*)."[44] But it was left to the contemporary existential phenomenologists and personalists to develop in more rich detail the indispensable role and unique characteristic of the I-Thou dialogue – as contrasted with the I-It dialogue with impersonal entities – in coming to know ourselves explicitly as persons, as "I." St. Thomas would have been delighted, I am sure, with such new developments in philosophy, and would have quickly integrated them into his own. These sensitive phenomenological descriptions have made it clear just how we come to the awareness of ourselves as "I" through the reaching out of another to us who is already an "I" and appeals to us to respond as another self, a "Thou," not merely as the stimulus-response of an impersonal thing but as another personal "I" self-consciously and freely open to the other. Unless someone else treats me as a "Thou" I can never wake up to myself as an "I," as a person. I am thinking here of the analyses of thinkers like Martin Buber, Gabriel Marcel, John Macmurray, Emmanuel Mounier and the Christian personalists, Jean-Paul Sartre, and many others, whom I got to know while studying for my Ph.D. in Louvain just after World War II.[45]

From all that the ancients knew, and we have learned since, of the social nature of the human person, it is clear that the entire development of personal life unfolds through active dialogue with an ever growing matrix of relations to other persons and the larger world beyond them. The growing child gets its self-confidence and sense of self-worth in response to the nurturing, caring love of its parents and immediate family and surrounding playmates – with all the chances of distortions and flaws in all these relationships, which can often leave permanent traces, both positive and negative, in the growing person's attitude toward itself and the world. Then the teenage person must struggle to find its own identity as distinct from its parents and in relation to its peers, especially of the opposite sex. So too the young adult must affirm itself and find its place in the vaster and more complex matrix of relations that is the adult world of ever-widening social communities, with possibilities of frustration, alienation, and isolation all along the way.

Everywhere our growth and development, positive and negative both, are mediated by relations – though not, we insist – simply reducible to them. No wonder that in the world of psychology and psychotherapy today the person is defined primarily, often exclusively, in relational terms. Finally, at the deepest level of its being and self-identity the human person must be defined in terms of its permanent relationship to God, the Source of all being, as the latter's created image. Who I am at my deepest level can only be understood in irreducibly relational terms: I am an *image of* God, brought into being by love, and called to transformation and final union *with* my Source. Mere introspection into my isolated inner consciousness loses itself finally in an impenetrable abyss of unlit mystery. Only the ultimate Light can light me up to myself at the deepest levels of my being and meaning.

In all of this apparently total immersion in relations to others, there is actually an alternating rhythm (or spiral movement, if you will) going on. Relations come into us and call us outward first; then we (should, normally) return to our own center to reflect on the result and integrate it into the abiding center of the self, expanding it and enriching it in the process. This permits the enriched self to then reach out further to others, with a surer and more profound sense of self-possession and ability to communicate and share our own riches. So the spiral of self-development should ideally go on, alternating harmoniously between the two poles of the person's being: self-possession and self-communication. As Josef

Pieper has put it with his usual felicity of phrase, commenting on a pregnant text of Thomas himself:

> The higher the form of intrinsic existence, the more developed becomes the relatedness with reality, also the more profound and comprehensive becomes the sphere of this relationship: namely, the world. And the deeper such relations penetrate the world of reality, the more intrinsic becomes the subject's existence.... These two aspects combined – dwelling most intensively within itself, and being *capax universi*, able to grasp the universe – together constitute the essence of the spirit. Any definition of "spirit" will have to contain these two aspects as its core.[46]

Translate "spirit" as "personalized spirit," or person as spirit, and he is making the same point as I am. Thus the life of every human person unfolds as a journey of the spirit through an ever-developing spiral circulation between self-presence and active self-expressive presence to others, between the "I" and the world, both personal and subpersonal, between inward-facing self-possession and outward-facing openness to the other. And, paradoxically, the more intensely I am present to myself at one pole, the more intensely I am present and open to others at the other. And reciprocally, the more I make myself truly present to the others as an "I" or self, the more I must also be present to myself, in order that it may be truly *I* that is present to them, not a mask.

The same creative tension exists, by the way, in the most fundamental relationship of all, that of the person to being itself. For the more I become aware of myself as related by intelligence and will to the whole order of being as intelligible and good, the more I come to understand myself as a human person, as embodied spirit, or "spirit-in-the-world"; and reciprocally, the more I come to take possession of myself as person, the more I wake up to my innate openness and orientation to the limitless horizon of being. Once again, to *be* is to be *substance-in-relation*.

Against this rich background of contemporary phenomenology's description of person as relational, let us now return to the metaphysical roots of the person in being itself as the act of existence (*esse*), in the hope of understanding more deeply this innate drive of the person toward joining with other beings in the community of relations.

In the first part of the lecture we developed the dynamic, self-communicating, relational aspect of every real being because of its act of existence (*esse*). But person for St. Thomas, as we have seen, is the highest, most intense expression of the perfection of being. There are, of course, varying levels of perfection within the order of personal being itself, once we have crossed the threshold dividing it from the sub-personal. We know of three: Infinite Perfection (God), finite pure spirits (angels), human beings as embodied spirits. It follows, then, that all we have said about this self-communicating aspect of being applies in the fullest, most developed way to the realm of persons.

Thus, a personalized being must obey the basic dyadic ontological structure of all being, that is, *presence in itself* and *presence to others*. But the outgoing, self-expressive, self-communicating, relational aspect must be an equally intrinsic and primordial aspect of every person as is its interiority and self-possession. And although there is a priority of order of the latter over the former, still each aspect is of equal worth and value. To be a person is to be intrinsically expansive, ordered toward self-manifestation and self-communication. This is the decisive advance over the Aristotelian substance, which was indeed, as nature, ordered toward action and reception, but, as form, was oriented primarily toward self-realization, the fulfillment of its own perfection as form, rather than sharing with others. The Neoplatonic dynamism of the self-diffusiveness of

the good as taken over by St. Thomas is needed to
expand this orientation toward action beyond the
self-centered viewpoint of form towards the wider
horizon of other persons and the universe as a
whole. To do justice to Aristotle, he himself
worked this in practice into his philosophy of man,
at least partially, in his notions of friendship and
the *polis*, the city-state, as the natural locus of
human flourishing. But he had no deep metaphysical grounding of this in his metaphysics of form
and substance and his separated spiritual sub-
stances, the celestial Prime Movers, are each
eternally locked in solitary self-contemplation.
This intrinsic expansiveness of the person towards
action and the relationality flowing from it, not
just for self-fulfillment but for communicating
one's own richness to others – both rooted in the
expansiveness of existence as intensive act – open
up a new perspective for viewing the meaning of
the person, in the universe. We are moving
towards a metaphysics of love.

Let us explore more in detail this relational
aspect of the human person, beginning from the
bottom up. The initial relationality of the human
person towards the outer world of nature and
other persons is primarily receptive, in need of
actualizing its latent potentialities from without.
The human person as child first goes out towards
the world as poor, as appealingly but insistently

needy. The primary response partner is the mother, who meets the growing person's needs ideally with caring love. First she responds to the physical and basic psychic needs, ·then slowly draws forth over the early years the active interpersonal response of the child as an I to herself as Thou, by her active relating to the child precisely as a loving I to a unique, special, and beloved Thou, not just as a useful or interesting object or thing, or another instance of human nature. John Macmurray has beautifully described the process of personalization, of drawing out of latent potentiality the self-conscious awareness and active-interpersonal response of the growing child-person, first by the mother or her surrogate, then by the father, the whole family, the neighborhood community, the school, etc.[47]

Thus the receptive dimension dominates at first in the development of the human person to full self-possession and self-manifestation. Then the active, freely initiated response side emerges more and more into full self-conscious actuality, enabling us, as we approach personal maturity, to advance *pari passu* with both sides of our being, giving and receiving, each supporting and being supported by the others. Thus we are caught up in, and give conscious expression to, the great, ongoing, alternating, dyadic rhythm of all existential being: in itself and towards-others, as though the whole universe itself were one great rhythm of breathing in and breathing out. The self-consciousness of a human person, then, does not start off in full, luminous self-presence. It begins rather in a kind of darkness, a state of being in potency toward knowing all beings, in act toward none. To actualize itself it must first open itself to the world of others, be waked up by their action on it and its own active response. Only then, through the mediation of the other, can it return fully to itself, as St. Thomas puts it, to discover itself as this unique human person.[48] And this process can come to fruition only by actively engaging in interpersonal relations with other human persons like me, who treat me as a Thou in an interpersonalist social matrix of I-Thou-We that constitutes the human community. Animals are incapable of this total return to self to become self-conscious. Hence they cannot be persons; they cannot say "I."

All this process of interaction, of giving and receiving, which constitutes the "breathing of being," we might say, necessarily spins out a whole web of relationality in all directions, growing more and more intricate as the lives of both individual persons and whole communities evolve. To be a person is to be related. The two, as in all being, are inseparable though not simply reducible. The *particular* individuals or things to

which I am in fact related in my life may indeed
be accidental (though not all, I believe): but the
fact that my being and its fulfillment are and must
be relational is intrinsic and essential to my very
being and personhood. As Charles Davis has put it
aptly:

> Man's true subjectivity is not the self-
> sufficient independence of an isolated
> monad, but a self-possessed openness to the
> plenitude of being. As an embodied
> subjectivity, the self participates in the
> plenitude of being only in and through the
> world with which it is bodily one.[49]

All the rich phenomenological analyses of our
time, such as of Merleau-Ponty on our being-in-
the-world through the body, and of the
interpersonalists on interpersonal dialogue, are
welcome here to fill in our general sketch.

Let us turn now to the more active side of the
relational dimension of the person, namely, its
self-communicative side. Clearly there is an
acquisitive side to our going out to others, because
we are poor and seeking our self-fulfillment. That
is all too obvious on the human scene. But in St.
Thomas's metaphysics of existential being there is
also a more generous drive toward self-
communication of one's own being because it is
positively rich – a carry-over from the old

Neoplatonic self-diffusiveness of the good. All beings below the human manifest this, as we have seen, at least in sharing energy in some form. And since this self-communication is a communication of being in some way, and being and goodness are convertible for Aquinas, such a self-communication always tends in some way toward the good, toward sharing the good that the communicator possesses. Now when this intrinsic dynamism toward self-communication is realized on the level of personal being as such it turns into a self-conscious, free self-communication. In a word, it turns into love in some form. Despite all the conflicting drives within our flawed human nature, it is still connatural for a human person to be a lover, to go out towards others we love, sharing what we have and wishing them the good they need for their own flourishing, for they too are good by a participation in being similar to our own.

To be an actualized human person, then, is to be a *lover*, to live a life of inter-personal self-giving and receiving. Person is essentially a "we" term. Person exists in its fullness only in the plural. As Jacques Maritain puts it with profound metaphysical and experiential insight in one of his most luminous passages:

Thus it is that when a man has been really awakened to the sense of being or existence, and grasps intuitively the obscure, living depth of the Self and subjectivity, he discovers by the same token the basic generosity of existence and realizes, by virtue of the inner dynamism of this intuition, that love is not a passing pleasure or emotion, but the very meaning of his being alive.[50]

Thus subjectivity reveals itself as "self-mastery for self-giving . . . by spiritual existing in the manner of a gift."[51]

So too another contemporary Thomist, who has tuned in powerfully to the dynamic, relational side of both being and person, Norbert Hoffman, speaks eloquently of "this movement of the *pro*, this self-openness to the other . . . [as] the primal mystery and the first of all impulses in the heart of being. All of its own, and not because of subsequent determination, being posits itself as *communicatio*; its essential form is called 'love.'"[52] Hoffman rightly traces this intrinsic property of all beings, and even more of persons, back to its ultimate source in divine being itself, whose very nature, as revealed to us in the Christian-doctrine of God as Triunely personal, turns out to be self-communicative, interpersonal love. We shall do the same later.

Just what is it, we might ask, that a person communicates in being *self*-communicative? We exchange, of course, all kinds of material goods. But for giving to be truly personalized, a gift must proceed from the deeper levels of the person as person, that is, as intellectually self-conscious and free, in a word, from the spiritual roots of the person. What the person really has to give, therefore, is from its spiritual treasury, from the two great inner resources that I would summarize broadly as wisdom and love – wisdom including the whole area of knowledge from practical know-how to the highest speculative and spiritual wisdom; love including the wide range of possible love relations. Both are mediated, of course, in endlessly diverse ways through the body and other material symbols. In sum, what one person can really give of itself to another really comes down to: wisdom, love, the joy of togetherness both in shared action and simple loving co-presence or communion, and the creative expression of all this in the many ways appropriate to an embodied spirit.

This expansive drive of the human person towards others tends to flow over naturally, if not blocked, into the formation of all kinds of human bonds, usually more or less interlaced with need, but not exclusively so. And these bonds in turn coalesce – as in the whole subhuman world too, into larger interlocking systems, which among

humans we call *community*. Here the whole philosophy and psychology of human community
finds its place to work out the details, which I cannot do here. Let me refer here only to the profound and creative work done by Mary Rousseau
on the personalist philosophical foundations of
human community in her recent book, *Community: The Tie That Binds*. There she finds the
living roots of every viable human community in
some kind of communion of love, involving an
altruistic component of self-giving, even self-
forgetting love of friendship – a rather daring
move in social philosophy, it seems to me. She and
I would agree, I think, that all being tends
ultimately towards communion, flaming up into
consciousness in persons.[53]

On this point there is no need to do a
"creative completion" of St. Thomas. In treating
of the perfection of the universe as a whole, he
affirms quite explicitly, in a great sweeping cosmic
vision, that the whole universe of subrational
beings exists for the sake of making possible and
nurturing the life of rational beings, and that the
final perfection of the latter is the "communication" (*communicatio*) between rational beings
themselves, in a word, the communion of persons,
first in this life and then in full completeness in
the next life by communion with God and the
community of all the blessed. In a word, the final

goal and perfection of the whole universe is, literally, the *communion between persons*, who in turn gather up the whole universe in their consciousness and love and thus lead it back to its Source.[54]

It is already well known that Thomas speaks of the power of the finite mind, including the human, to gather up and "inscribe the whole order of the universe" in the unity of its own consciousness, "as a remedy for its finitude." But it is not as well known that he also went further and declared that because of the bond of the rest of the universe with rational beings as its fulfillment, it is possible to love with the altruistic love of charity not only other persons but the whole material universe itself! The new perspective opened on ecology and care for the earth is a rich one. It is hard to conceive of a more radically personalized universe than this.[55]

And the remarkable paradox in all this is that we do not lose our self-identity and self-possession as we become absorbed deeply in communion and community. Belonging to an authentic community does not submerge the free self but liberates it, nourishes it as its natural environment and ends up bringing us to know our own unique individuality even more keenly. (Inauthentic community can, however, all too easily submerge and diminish the self and its dignity, as we all know.)

Many social thinkers today feel that the truly successful corporations and businesses of tomorrow will be those who have learned this lesson well. Karl Rahner has expressed powerfully this vital tension and complementarity between person and community in the light of the universal dynamics of all being:

> At first sight one is inclined to say that anything that exists possesses its own peculiarity (and difference) in inverse relation to its unity with, its bond with what is other than itself; that, in other words, it decreases in selfhood the more it is bound up with something else, while any growth in distinguishing selfhood involves a decrease in unity and relationship to anything other than itself. It is no exaggeration to say that this error, seemingly such a self-evident truth, the apparent contradiction between all-embracing unity and individual uniqueness, lies at the root of all the errors and heresies that have arisen in the study of relationships, of social being. And yet even at the lowest subhuman level, if we look at it properly, we see that it is not so. Something that is merely separated from something else is neither really anything for itself (does not really possess anything for itself) nor really one with anything else. . . . Hence

the true law of things is not: the more special and distinct in character the more separated, isolated and discontinuous from anything else, but the reverse: the more really
special a thing is, the more abundance of
being it has in itself, the more intimate
unity and mutual participation there will be
between it and what is other than itself.[56]

To *be*, therefore, it finally turns out, is to *be-
in-communion*, or if you wish, to be, in the full
deployment of its actuality, is to *commune* with
one's fellow existents, and the most intense and
luminous manifestation of this shines forth in the
life of the person, as self-conscious, free, communion with other persons. Where this is missing,
the authentic actualization of the person will be
more or less severely stunted or distorted by inef-
fective substitutes (power, possessions, etc.).
There is no viable substitute for communion; this
is the law of being itself.

5. Receptivity as Complementary to Self-communication

There remains one last piece to be developed
in the metaphysics of being and the person as self-
communicative. This is the other complementary
side of the metaphysics of being, and especially
the person, as active, expansive, self-communica-

ting – a side that has not found explicit development at all, as a *positive perfection* of being, in the
metaphysics of St. Thomas and Thomism in general, so far as I know, although it is certainly
implicit in his phenomenology of friendship. I am
speaking of *receptivity* as a positive perfection of
being.

Already in the first part of this lecture we
took up the point briefly, as a necessary complement to the self-comunicative aspect of all being.
If there is to be effective self-communication of
any being, there must be a corresponding
receptivity for it somewhere in being, otherwise
the process would be aborted from the start. In a
word, there can be no giving without receiving.
Ordinarily metaphysicians, including St. Thomas,
following the lead of Aristotle, have identified
receptivity with the deficiency side of being, i.e.,
with poverty, potentiality, a prior lack that is later
filled up. Pure actuality seems to exclude
receptivity, as indeed it does for Aristotle.

There is no great harm perhaps, in looking at
the subhuman world this way, since there is so
much truth in it due to the ubiquitous element of
change, passage from potentiality to act, that is
always involved in that dimension of being –
though even there one suspects that that is not the
whole story in the world of the new physics. But
once one crosses the threshold into personal

being, the picture begins to change significantly. Once one begins to analyze love, in particular the highest mode of love, the love of pure friendship, it is clear that *mutuality* is of the essence of this love. Friendship means essentially that one's love is accepted, joyfully welcomed by another, and returned in kind, and the same is true reciprocally for the other person with respect to me. Receptivity, therefore, is part of the essence of the highest love.

Here the ontological value of receptivity, as not a defect or inferiority but a positive perfection of being, emerges more and more clearly into the light. There is indeed a side of imperfection included, insofar as change is involved, that is, a passage from prior non-possession of my friend's love to later receiving it, or from potentiality to act. But if we carefully analyze this, it becomes clear that this imperfection is solely due to the change or temporal aspect, not to the very nature of receptivity as such, which at the level of personal love is not passivity at all but an active, welcoming receptivity, that is purely positive in nature, a relation of act to act rather than of act to potency. Receptivity and passivity are not identical. As Gerard O'Hanlon puts it admirably:

This is shown most clearly at the top of an ascending scale of subject/object relationships in the created sphere when one arrives at the interpersonal relationship between two subjects, at the heart of which is a welcoming, active receptivity. . . . the higher up the scale of created reality one goes the more this passivity (in the sense of an active receptivity) increases, and the more it may be seen, in the case of human inter-personal encounter, as a perfection.[57]

To make this clear, all we have to do is to remove in thought the aspect of motion and change. Thus if person A timelessly gives perfection X to person B, then B does not first lack perfection and then later receive it, but *always* possesses it in *act*. And if we add that B receives X in equal fullness to A's possession of it, then no potency is involved at all. There is only the possession of perfection X plus the purely positive relationship of active, grateful welcoming of it as a gift from A. In a word, the love relationship, if properly understood, opens up the capital metaphysical and psychological insight that to be gifted and to be grateful are in themselves not a sign of inferiority or deficiency at all, but part of the splendor and wonder of being itself at its highest actualization, that is, being as communion. In a word, self-communication and receptivity are two complementary and inseparable sides of the dynamic process of being itself, implicit in St.

Thomas's own notion of *esse* as primal expansive act and perfection.

I would be the first to admit, however, that one cannot find the above development at all explicitly in St. Thomas's metaphysics, and *a fortiori* not in Aristotle's. That is why I spoke of this lecture as a "creative completion" of St. Thomas. Where does this new insight come from? I admit that I have never developed it before in my own writings on St. Thomas, nor have I seen it in other Thomists, though I am open to correction here. Process thinkers like Hartshorne, Cobb, and Ford have been nudging me towards it for years, and I have been nibbling sympathetically, but cautiously, because I could not get the metaphysical roots clear. But the principal catalytic agent, to which I am happy to admit my full indebtedness, is the profound and daring speculation of the Swiss Catholic theologian, Hans Urs von Balthasar, on the Christian notion of God as personally Triune and as the supreme model of what it means to be.[58] For here we do have a case, transcending our own human experience, but revealed to us by the Source itself, of where being as receptivity is present in the Son and the Spirit at its most intense, as a pure perfection of existence at its highest, and hence of *absolutely equal ontological worth and value* with being as self-communicative. For it is part of the revealed doctrine of God as

Trinity that the Second and Third Persons are of absolutely equal ontological perfection as the Father. Thus within the unity of the Supreme Being the Father is subsistent Self-Communication, while the Son is subsistent Receptivity (the Holy Spirit as well in its own unique mode), but both aspects are equally valuable and integral to what it means to *be* at its most intense. The highest instance of being is a unity that is not solitary, like Plotinus's One, but *Communion*.

Here we see in the most striking way how a specifically *Christian* philosophy can fruitfully shed light on a philosophical problem itself, by drawing on Revelation. The light from Revelation does not operate strictly as the premise for a philosophical argument, properly speaking, but operates as opening up for reflection a new possibility in the nature and meaning of being that we might never have thought of ourselves from our limited human experience, but which, once opened up, is so illuminating that it now shines on its own as an insight into the nature of being and persons that makes many things suddenly fall into place whose depths we could not fathom before. More and more in recent years I have come to realize that the doctrine of the Trinity is a uniquely powerful source of illumination in both the philosophy of being and the philosophy of the person. We do not have time here to develop the numerous fruitful implications of the doctrine of the Trinity as a paradigm for human relations in community, as a number of contemporary Christian thinkers are now doing. Appreciating more fully the complementary values of both masculine and feminine is only one of these implications.

We are now in a position to step back and view this whole analysis of the expansive, self-communicative aspect of the person (and of being) in a new light. We have tried to show so far how the dynamism of self-communication is part of the very nature of being and so of the person. But the metaphysician would like to probe further, if he can, into *why* all this should be the case. I think we now have the answer: the reason why all being, and all persons preeminently, are such is precisely because that is the way the Supreme Being, the Source of all being, actually is, and, since all creatures – and in a special way persons – are participations and hence images of their divine Source, then it follows that all created beings, and more intensely persons, will mirror in some characteristic way the divine mode of being. As the doctrine of the Trinity reveals, God's very nature is to be self-communicative love. "God is love," St. John tells us. And the wonderful consequence is that we can now see that it is of the very nature of being as such, at its highest, i.e., as personal, to be such. This is what it really means to *be* at its fullest: to be caught up in the great dynamic process of self-communication, receptivity, and return that we have called *communion*. For that is the way the Source of beings *is* and we, his creatures, cannot but tend to be like our Source as far as we can. It is fighting our own deepest drive to try to live otherwise and still become authentic, fulfilled persons. "Let us make man to our image and likeness," as *Genesis* told us long ago. Our whole destiny is to fulfill the image latent within us and draw it out, as the Greek Fathers put it beautifully, into manifest likeness.

It is worth noting how far this conception of the human person is from the excessively autonomous, individualistic one of John Locke and so many modern Western political thinkers since Descartes, where the primary value is not put on relationship and communion but on self-sufficiency as far as possible, protection of one's person and property from the intrusions of others, etc. These things are indeed important, up to a point in a realistic view of human society as it is, with all its imperfections. But there is a radical change of perspective when these become paramount and overshadow the interpersonal sharing dimension. In a word, it is impossible to make justice alone the foundation for a viable social

order. Only friendship, altruistic love of some
kind, can supply the positive cohesive energy
required, as St. Thomas himself maintains.

Before passing on to the next section, I would
like to highlight briefly one aspect of the
expansive, self-communicative aspect of the person we have outlined above. It is part of the overall expansive movement, but deserves special
attention for its importance in the coming to self-
knowledge and self-actualization of the person.

This is the aspect of the person as self-
manifesting, self-expressive. All throughout being,
the drive towards action includes a drive toward
self-revelation, self-manifestation, self-expression
through action. Every action in some way is self-
revelatory of the active center from which it
proceeds. As St. Thomas tells us over and over,
the operation of a being manifests its existence
and points out (*indicat*) its nature or essence.[59]
The substantial forms of things in themselves are
hidden from us, but they shine forth through the
doors (*ostia*) of their accidents and operations.[60]
One might well say that action and its implications
is the primary key to the whole epistemology of
Aquinas. All knowledge of the real for him is an
interpretation of action. I know my own self
because and insofar as I act. I know other things
because, and insofar as, they act on me, with all
the implications thereof. The cutting of the bridge

of action as the self-revelation of being is, to my mind, the single greatest flaw in modern classical epistemology from Descartes on, culminating disastrously in the epistemology of Immanuel Kant.

So too even more so for the person. It is connatural for us, giving full expression to the dynamism of existence flowing through us at its most intense as personalized, to reveal, manifest, express ourselves to other persons, to make manifest who we are, what we believe in, stand for etc., in a word, "our story." Only when we express ourselves to others – including God, of course, who is infinitely self-expressive in his Word, the Son, and the Holy Spirit – can we come to know our own selves fully. As we mentioned earlier in speaking of self-possession, we do not start off in luminous self-understanding but must go out to the world and other persons first, then return to know ourselves by reflecting on our actions, whether and how they express who and what we really are or would like to be.

Since it is the nature, then, of all being to reveal and express itself, it seems that if we do not do this, if we keep our interior selves locked up within us unexpressed to anyone, our very being will be diminished. "Every real substance exists for the sake of its operations," St. Thomas tells us, which are "the goal and perfection of the substance itself."[61] What we do not express in any way from our inner being will tend to get sedimented over, sink further and further into obscurity, so that finally it becomes no longer available to us even within, and becomes as though it is not. Or indeed, if something negative, it can grow into a monster, corroding us from within.

It is of great importance, then, for a healthy personal development to find some appropriate way of expressing to *somebody* all the significant levels of being and personality within us, including the deepest and most intimate. In fact, this is one of the things that is most appreciated and treasured when we share it with others – when we share "our story" with others, and receive theirs in return. Paradoxically, it seems that what we don't share, we tend to lose hold of. In the realm of the person, what we don't give away we can't hold on to. Someone may object, "I share my deepest secrets with God, and that is enough." That is certainly an excellent start. And in the realm of negative secrets it may well be enough. But in the realm of our positive riches, it still seems to me better, more in accord with the drive of being itself coursing through us, to give also some expression to this interior world in a manner appropriate to our status as *embodied* spirits, i.e., by some sensible or externally expressed symbol, word or otherwise. Thus human beings have always tended to come together to express the deepest level within them, their religious beliefs, by shared liturgical worship, symbolic by essence.

Authentic self-expression, however, does not mean just that we do a lot of talking. Psychologists tell us that Americans tend to be roughly 75% extroverts, 25% introverts. So it seems a little harder for us to talk about deep private things within us than some others. But it is important to make a real effort to do so, so that nothing of major significance within us, especially all our positive aspirations, remains totally unexpressed.

Why it should be that way, that self-possession must keep pace with self-expression, is one of the deep mysteries of being. Again the most illuminating explanation comes from the Christian revelation of the Trinity. It is the case that the Supreme Source of all being is precisely that way. The Father expresses himself with total infinite fullness in his Son, the *Word*, and both again in the Holy Spirit. It is the very nature of God, the supreme exemplar of what it means to be, to be self-expressive. And that is why we, his images must be also, if we too are to *be* and be *persons fully. The image in us cries out to be made manifest.*

6. Personal Being as Self-Transcending

We now come to the last of the three phases of personal development, and the one most shot through with mystery and paradox – but also with splendor. This is the requirement that the fully developed person be *self-transcending.* Here we can pick up St. Thomas again without too much creative completion required, since much of this point has already been explicitly developed by him, or is evidently implicit in much that he has said, and needs only for the parts to be drawn together into a whole.[62]

Already in the first section of this lecture on being as dynamic, expansive act we briefly indicated how all existing beings tend to reach beyond themselves to form larger unities, etc., and in a sense how every finite being, as participating imperfectly in the Infinite Good, tends implicitly in some way to imitate and move toward the Infinite Good in its own appropriate way, insofar as its limiting essence allows, although only personal being, as spiritual, can attain direct union with this good. Now we consider this great hidden inner movement of all created being as it bursts into full explicit consciousness as self-conscious and free on the level of person. It is here that we see clearly the full meaning of the whole restless movement of the cosmos up through evolution toward man and beyond toward the "Omega

Point," as Teilhard de Chardin puts it. For, as Thomas Berry expresses it eloquently: "Man is that being in whom the grand diversity of the universe celebrates itself consciously."[63] We have time here only to sketch the outlines of this rich dimension of self-transcendence, which moves finally from the articulation of metaphysics into the silence of mysticism, and links up Thomistic metaphysics and philosophical anthropology with all the great spiritual traditions.

There is first a very wide meaning to the term "self-transcending," according to which any person who goes out of himself to relate himself to another in knowledge or love can be said to be self-transcending in a horizontal sense. It is really only another technical term for the relation of intentionality toward another than oneself, a term brought in by the existentialists (Heidegger, Sartre, etc.), but whose content is really as old as the ancient and medieval intentionality analysis of knowledge and love. All knowing and loving of another is in this sense a transcending of one's own self and limits. This meaning is not our concern at present, important though it is for the full analysis of the life of personal being.

Then there is the more restricted sense of the term according to which every time we reach out to love and care for another for the other's own sake we are transcending ourselves, leaving behind our own natural self-centeredness to put our center of attention in another. All authentic friendship and love of benevolence is a self-transcending act in this sense. Important as it is, I do not think I need to dwell at length on this point. I believe it is clear enough to all of us that no one can reach mature development as a person without the experience of opening oneself, giving oneself to another in self-forgetting love of some kind. To be a true self, one must somehow go out of oneself, forget oneself. This apparent paradox is an ancient one and has been noted over and over in the various attempts to work out philosophies of love and friendship down the ages. St. Thomas develops it succinctly but clearly in his analysis of natural friendship and supernatural charity.

Just how to resolve this paradox and render intelligible the going out of oneself as necessary to be fully oneself is a profound and difficult philosophical problem, at least to resolve conceptually. St. Thomas's solution lies along the lines of participation and similitude. First because we participate in the same human nature with other human persons, secondly because we all share in the common bond of existence that bonds together all real existents, and finally because we are all images of God, bearing the stamp of the same original Source, the pure subsistent fullness of existence, we recognize a deep natural affinity between ourselves and others as though they were somehow other selves, complementary completions of our own limited being as the innate desire unfolds within us to possess with intellect and will the whole infinite plenitude of existence that we can never capture within the limits of our own finite essences by ourselves. It is our implicit love of the infinite that grounds all our love of the imperfect and incomplete images that are all finite beings.[64]

Another, and more dynamic, aspect of the solution, stemming from our perfection rather than our imperfection, is that as images of God we too must imitate in our own way the ecstatic, outgoing self-sharing of God as Infinite Good. Personal development in a created person is to become more and more like God. And since the self-diffusiveness of the Good in a supremely personal being like God is nothing else than love, then God is Love, the infinite Lover, and we too, as his images must be lovers. So the ultimate mystery of being turns out to be that *to be* is *to be a lover*, as we developed earlier.

I could develop this rich vein further. But important as it is, I believe it is already familiar enough to you so that I can push on to explore self-transcendence at its most radical and intense level, where the mystery and paradox of personal being become most profound, liberating, and beautiful. This involves a profound, abiding shift in the attitude of a person toward the world, a movement of self-transcendence not just in a horizontal but in a *vertical sense*.

What I am talking about is a radical *decentering of consciousness* from self to God, where the main focus of our conscious interest and concern is no longer ourselves and our own self-development, even in the good sense of this term. We are drawn out of ourselves, called now to focus on the Great Center beyond us – also within us, of course – to take as our own center the One Center and Source of the whole universe, of all being and goodness, the Great Self, if you wish. The central focus of my concern is now not just with my good or that of my family, friends, etc., but the Good in itself and the good of the whole universe as seen from God's point of view. In a word, we take on a God's eye view of all things, seeing them as he sees them in the ordered unity of being as a whole, and loving them all as he loves them in the ordered unity of goodness as a whole. Even my own self I now love, no longer as the implicit center of the universe (which is at first our natural attitude – each person is the center of the world for himself), but only *as known and loved by God*, in my place in the whole scheme of things. In a word, I know and love

myself as God knows and loves me. And as a
result I open my whole being to the Great Center,
so that it can act out its life of creative love
through me. This decentering of self, this putting
off or loss of self, as it has been called in many
spiritual traditions, turns out then to become, in a
marvelous lived paradox, a new finding of one's
true self at a deeper level. As St. Paul put it with
lapidary density, "I live, now not I, but Christ lives
in me" (Gal 2:20). (From this it should be clear,
pace the Buddhists, that the "self" that is put off
is not the radical ontological self, but the self-
centered self, the *self-centered mode of consciousness.*)

What is the dynamo behind this ecstatic
decentering movement? It is the pull of the
Infinite Good, drawing the whole person as finite
spirit toward the total fulfillment it longs for, at
first implicitly, finally more explicitly, by union
with the Infinite Good. This is the deep finality
built into the very nature of every finite being as
spirit, endowed with intellect and will, which can
be satisfied only by the total plenitude of being as
true (intelligible), good, and beautiful. Although
every finite being implicitly tends toward the
Infinite Good by imitating and imaging it in some
way, and there is also clearly an immense inner
groping movement of the material world upwards
toward spirit through evolution – a movement

itself not explicable by chance – still only a spiritual being can pick up this ontological striving, turn it into self-conscious love, and carry the rest of the universe with it all the way to direct personal union with the Infinite Good that is the lodestar of all being.

Thus there is always an expansive drive within the act of existence wherever it is found. Where found in infinite fullness in God, it tends to pour over ecstatically in timeless, perfect, loving self-communication within the divine nature itself, in the immanent dynamic of the three divine Persons, called by the Fathers *circumincessio* ("circular movement" or procession within): from the Father to the Son to the Holy Spirit, then back again through the Son to the Father, in an intense, timeless, always completed yet always going on, ecstasy of intercommunion. Then this inner fullness pours over again freely to share its goodness in finite creation. This is the outgoing impetus of being. Then the infinite Source draws all creatures back to itself by the pull of the good working proportionately within the nature of each, since no finite nature can actually exist without its nature (as existent, possessing its own act of *esse*) being intrinsically finalized toward the good. This is what a nature *means* for St. Thomas. Thus there is a great double "movement" in the universe of actual being from the Source outward toward creation and from creation back towards its Source. St. Thomas calls this the great circle of being (*circulatio entium*), the exodus of the Many from the One, and the return home again of the Many to the One.[65] Being is always intrinsically "on the move," it seems, both within and without God. We as finite persons actually manifest both aspects, both the ecstatic sharing, in imitation of our Source, because we are rich, and the ecstatic going out of ourselves in longing search for fulfillment, because we are poor.

Once our turning toward the Source, the Great Center, has become fully conscious and freely chosen, so that we take it explicitly now as *the* Center of our own lives in vertical self-transcendence, a process Bernard Lonergan calls falling in love with God, then at this point the natural process of self-development of the person undergoes a kind of reversal. Although the phases of human development are by no means watertight, rigidly demarcated from each other in a linear sequence, still the main thrust of development has been up to now from below upwards: from childhood to mature adulthood, advancing through growing self-possession, active self-communication, and self-transcendence on a horizontal level towards other human beings. But as we move more and more into the phase of vertical self-transcendence, putting off our self-centered consciousness to open up the Great Center and its transforming power, then a profound reversal in the movement of self-development takes place: it now flows primarily from above downwards, transforming us from above. As Lonergan puts it:

> Such transforming love has its occasions, its conditions, its causes. But once it comes and as long as it lasts, it takes over. One no longer is one's own. Moreover, in the measure that this transformation is effective, development comes not merely from below upwards but more fundamentally from above downwards. There has begun a life in which the heart has reasons which reason does not know. There has been opened up a new world in which the old adage, "Nothing is loved unless it is first known," yields to a new truth, "Nothing is truly known unless it is first loved." It is such transforming love than enables Paul to say: "The life I now live is not my life, but the life which Christ lives in me" (Gal 2:20).[66]

Something like this has been taught in all the great spiritual traditions. Jesus has warned us that "only he who loses himself will find himself." One of the central teachings of the Buddha is the "no-self" doctrine, which, if we get behind its later metaphysical interpretations, seems to have meant

primarily a spiritual attitude of radical selfless-
ness, such that the letting go of self mysteriously
releases the springs of deep, universal love and
compassion for all living things, even though no
mention is made of a higher Self or divine principle. In Hindu Advaita Vedanta, the *Atman* or
individual self finally lets go the illusion of its
separateness and becomes one with the *Atman* or
Great Self. The Sufi mystics become so
intoxicated with the love of God that they beg
God to "take away this I that stands between me
and Thee."[67]

This type of vertical self-transcendence is
obviously not the ordinary mode of consciousness
of every person who has reached psychological
maturity, though many more slip quietly into it, I
suspect, than are self-consciously aware of it. It is
a phase in the journey toward full self-
development as a person that usually emerges
somewhere toward mid-life, though for some who
are particularly generous and spiritually awake it
can be woven into their lives earlier, or even be
concentrated in a dramatic conversion-type experience. But more ordinarily, as Carl Jung has so
insightfully outlined in his theory of individuation
and integration, the first part of a person's life is
focused primarily on one's own self-development,
on the discovery and actualization of one's own
basic potentialities and skills, on affirming oneself

and establishing one's position in the world, in a word, on acquiring a strong and secure sense of self and what it can do. But once this sense of self and what it can do is securely established, some-where around the mid-point of our life's journey, sometimes earlier, sometimes later, a kind of call comes to us from our own depths – or beyond – sometimes clear, more often obscure. We come to realize that our self-development cannot go on to full term if we continue living the same way. To move on further some radical shift of focus must take place. This is the call to radical self-transcendence, to let go of our own selves as cen-ter of interest and take on the Great Center as our own new center of consciousness and open ourselves to let its life flow through us and express itself more and more fully in our lives. A profound transformation of our lives now occurs, so that we begin to shine forth more and more as images of God's own loving presence making itself known on earth. And now our self-communication to others becomes, mysteriously, more and more of a God-communication through us.

This movement towards self-transcendence, however, is not an automatic one. Some heed the call and keep growing, discovering their deeper or "true selves" in the process. Some do not; they stagnate, wonder what is wrong with them now that the old ways of self-fulfillment no longer seem to work as effectively as before; they become restless, wander on the horizontal level looking for new challenges, new stimuli that will fill the mysterious void they feel developing, but avoiding the shift to a new self-transcending level of consciousness that will allow them to move forward again. Others more or less consciously and deliberately cling tenaciously to their self-centered ego, for fear of giving up "being in charge" of their lives and surrendering their wills to another, with the attendant implications for their life-style to which they have become attached; thus they positively block the flow of the Transcendent Center in them and through them, with the final consequence of stagnation or perhaps even disintegration of the self-development they have achieved.

Why is it that such a paradoxical decentering and letting go of self on the conscious level is necessary in order that any finite person may be able to go on to his or her full self-development? Can philosophy be of any help to us here? I think it can. The answer, insofar as it can be conceptualized, lies in the nature of spiritual intellect and will as dynamic faculties oriented by a built-in natural drive toward the fullness of their formal object, being and goodness as such.

Every created spiritual intellect, angelic, human, or whatever, is endowed according to St. Thomas, with a radical innate drive toward the whole of being, the unlimited horizon of being as intelligible. Now since the Source and fullness of all being is Infinite Being, there is in every spiritual intellect a natural drive to know God as Source, fullness of being, and final goal of all knowing, and also, included in this, to know all other things from his point of view, as he himself is, a natural drive in us as images of God to transcend our own limited point of view in knowing and take on his total one as far as is possible for us.

So too in the order of spiritual will there is a natural drive toward all being as good, the unlimited horizon of goodness as such. Now here too, since God is the Source, center, and fullness of all goodness, there is a natural drive to love him as Infinite Goodness beyond all other goods, even ourselves, and also, included implicitly in this, to love all other goods as he himself loves them, from his point of view. Thus we are drawn to transcend our own limited, self-absorbed perspective of loving to love and care for the whole universe, for the whole order of goods as they truly exist and are loved by him in ordered unity around himself as Center. And this includes loving my own self, no longer as the center of my focus, but as I truly am, and am known and loved by him, within this total order. I now wish, as far as I can, to put off my own and take on God's point of view by knowing, evaluating, loving caring for all things, including myself, as he does.

Here shines forth the magnificent, liberating paradox of personal development: because the person is endowed with a spiritual intellect and will, possessing a natural drive toward the infinite, the fullness of truth and goodness, the only way it can reach its own fullness of perfection as spirit is precisely to transcend its own – and any other – limited viewpoint to take on the divine point of view for knowing and loving all things, including itself. Only by de-centering ourselves, transcending our finite selves (in consciousness, of course, not in our essential being) to take on the Infinite Center, the authentic Center of all being, as our own center and perspective of knowing and loving all things, including ourselves, can we fully become our own true selves as embodied spirits and thus fulfill completely the potentialities of personal being as such. The fullness of personal development turns out to be a losing or letting go of oneself that is simultaneously and by that very fact a new finding of oneself at a deeper level. Self-transcendence is thus of the very essence of all personal development at its highest, whether the person involved identifies explicitly his new

Center as God or not. Only by reaching beyond the human can we succeed in becoming fully human. To refuse to do so condemns us to fall short of the human itself. To *be* a human person fully means to self-transcend toward the Infinite.[68]

7. The Problem of Evil

So far we have painted what is admittedly a very positive, optimistic view of what it means to be a human person. This is because we have been talking about the link between person and being, and being itself, for St. Thomas, insofar as it actually is, is always something positive and good. And the splendor of actual being does indeed shine forth at its brightest in the person. Evil is always the privation in a good being of some good that should be there. It is the hole in the cheese of being, to put it in homely terms. Still, what of all the obvious evil, alienation, stunted development we see in the actual human world around us?

This is all too evident, and brings into focus the other, shadow side of the created human person, which makes our actual historical world a *chiaroscuro* of light and shadow, like a Rembrandt painting. The human person is endowed with freedom, hence is intrinsically *defectible*, capable not only of rising to the heights but also of falling to the depths. Therefore all along the way the drive toward positive, ideal development built into the nature of the person as the standard-bearer of being can be blocked, frustrated, sabotaged, both from within and at least partly from without. Thus instead of mature self-possession we can have a negative, weak, alienated self-image; instead of responsible self-government we can have a retreat from moral responsibility, letting our wills be other-directed instead of inner-directed. Instead of loving self-communication and sharing we can have fearful, self-enclosed secretiveness, or a habit of going out to others only to get as much as possible from them or dominate them for our own advancement. Instead of authentic self-transcendence, especially vertical, we can have radical uncaring self-centeredness, so that instead of setting our compass on going home to the Great Center we can take as our only home our own needy, lonely selves.

The human journey toward our authentic Home is one that must be freely undertaken and navigated, with the ever-present possibility of wandering off course, either temporarily or perhaps even permanently. Reaching home in good shape is not an automatic process, but a high-stakes, high-risk achievement. But it does not make the journey less noble a one or the splendor of the person as pinnacle of being less bright. And there is help, both from downstairs and Upstairs,

so that the journey is less daunting – and shot
through with hope.

Conclusion

We have now come to the end of our journey
of exploration of the profound links between person and being for St. Thomas. Profoundly inspired
by Thomas's own explicit metaphysics of being
and the person, and gratefully stimulated by the
rich contemporary analyses of the relationality
and interpersonal aspects of human life, plus
recent theological speculation on the immensely
illuminating implications of the Christian revelation of God as Trinity, we have attempted a
"creative completion" of St. Thomas's own work.
This has been carried out partly by bringing
together various parts of his thought which he
himself did not explicitly link up but which seem
to me clearly implicit in the dynamism of his
thought and just waiting to be done, although he
himself, by historical chance, did not get around
to doing so. Occasionally, but rarely, we have gone
beyond what he himself seems even implicitly to
have thought, but I believe lies inevitably within
the dynamism of his own inexhaustibly rich
metaphysics of existential being (*esse*) as
expansive act.

The basic steps in the creative exploration have been: *I. The Nature of Being*, understood with the act of existence (*esse*) at its core, as dynamic, expansive act, first present in itself as "first act," then naturally pouring over in a "second act" to present itself to others in self-expression, self-communication, etc. through action. This action, which puts it in touch with the rest of the universe, generates a whole web of relations around it, outgoing and incoming, by interacting with others. Thus, since any being reaches its perfection only by its operation, and all self-communicative action generates relations, relationality becomes an equally primordial dimension of reality as substantiality. All beings tend toward forming associations with others into unified systems or communities. Thus to be is to be oriented towards relations and ultimately towards community. The new element here is the highlighting of the relational aspect of being, too often submerged in the tradition to the primacy of substance.

II. Transfer to the Person. Since the person is not something added onto being from the outside, but is the highest perfection and most intense expression of existential being itself, the person takes on more intensely the whole dynamism of existence as expansive, self-communicating act, now raised to the order of self-consciousness and freedom. So the person too becomes intrinsically oriented, towards self-expression and self-communication to others, hence towards relations and community, ultimately towards communion. To be a person is to *be with* . . . , to be a sharer, a receiver, a lover. Ultimately the reason why all this is so is that this is the very nature of the Supreme Being, the Source of all being, as revealed to us in the Christian doctrine of God as three Persons within the unity of one being, so that the very being of God is to be self-communicative love. This dynamism is then echoed in all of us, his creatures, and in a preeminent way in created persons.

Thus the Christian revelation of the Trinity is not some abstruse doctrine for theologians alone but has a unique illuminating power as to the meaning of being itself which carries metaphysical vision beyond what was accessible to it unaided. This is Christian philosophy at its most fruitful.

Finally the three basic phases of personal development, corresponding to the attributes of existential being itself, are self-possession, self-communication with its corollary of active receptivity as a positive perfection of being, significantly understressed by St. Thomas himself, and self-transcendence. To be a person is to be a dynamic act of existence on the move, towards self-conscious, free sharing and receiving, becoming a lover, and finally a lover totally centered on

Infinite Being and Goodness itself, the final goal of our journey as embodied spirits towards *being-as-communion* – the very nature of the Source of all being, and hence of all beings created in its image. Perhaps we can risk here a final summing up of all our exploration into person and being: to *be* fully a person consists in living out to the full the alternating rhythm of *self-possession* and *openness to others*, or, as Maritain put it, "self-mastery for self-giving"; for it is in the spark that passes from one of these poles to the other and back again that lies the secret of all authentic personal growth, creativity, life, and love that make the living person the supreme manifestation and glory of being. We might add that as this life unfolds in depth the two poles can even mysteriously come to interpenetrate one another, without losing their distinctness. Thus it is precisely – and only – through the person that the One and the Many – the oldest and the most profound mystery of all being – can finally be reconciled. Happy journey to my readers towards the full actualization of your own inestimable gift of personhood!

Notes

1. Cf. the interesting article by Robert Connor, "Relation, the Thomistic *Esse*, and American Culture: Toward a Metaphysic of Sanctity," *Communio* 17 (1990), 455-64, and other pieces in the same issue.

2. Josef Ratzinger, *Introduction to Christianity* (New York: Herder & Herder, 1970), pp. 132, 137; also the longer development in "Concerning the Notion of Person in Theology," *Communio* 17 (1990), 438-54.

3. W. Norris Clarke, "Action as the Self-Revelation of Being: A Central Theme in the Thought of St. Thomas," in Linus Thro, ed. *History of Philosophy in the Making* (Lantham, MD: University Press of America, 1982), pp. 63-80.

4. *Summa contra Gentes* I, ch. 43.

5. *Summa contra Gentes* II, ch. 7.

6. *De potentia* q. 2, art. 1.

7. *Summa contra Gentes* III, ch. 64.

8. *Summa Theologiae* I, q. 19, art. 2.

9. *Summa Theologiae* I, q. 105, art. 5.

10. *Summa contra Gentes* III, ch. 113.

11. Etienne Gilson, *Being and Some Philosophers* (Toronto: Pontifical Institute of Mediaeval Studies, 1952), p. 184.

12. Gerald Phelan, "The Existentialism of St. Thomas," *Selected Papers* (Toronto: Pontifical Institute of Mediaeval Studies, 1967), p. 77.

13. Jacques Maritain, *Existence and the Existent* (Garden City: Doubleday, 1957), p. 90.

14. Joseph de Finance, S.J., *Etre et agir dans la philosophie de S. Thomas* (Rome: Università Gregoriana, 1960).

15. All this is developed more fully in my article, "Action as the Self-Revelation of Being," see note 3.

16. I have developed this theme more fully in my article, "To Be is To Be Substance-in-Relation," in *Metaphysics as Foundation: Essays in Honor of Ivor Leclerc* (Albany: SUNY Press, 1992).

17. Joself Pieper, *The Truth of All Things*, reprinted in *Living the Truth* (San Francisco: Ignatius Press, 1989), pp. 83 and 82.

18. Gerard O'Hanlon, S.J., *The Immutability of God in the Theology of Hans Urs von Balthasar* (New York: Cambridge University Press, 1990). A very useful condensation of the book can be found in the same author's article, "Does God Change? Hans Urs von Balthasar on the Immutability of God," *Irish Theological Quarterly* 53 (1987), 161-83.

19. See the beautiful sweep of chapters developing this in St. Thomas, *Summa contra Gentes* III, chs. 16-21.

20. *Summa Theologiae* I, q. 29, art. 3.

21. Cf. C. De Vogel, "The Concept of Personality in Greek and Christian Thought," in J. Ryan, ed., *Studies in Philosophy and the History of Philosophy* (Washington: Catholic University of America Press, 1963), II, 20-60. See also the fine article "Person" by M. Müller, A. Lois Halder, J. Moller (philosophy), A. Sand (Scripture), and K. Rahner (theology) in *Sacramentum Mundi: An Encyclopedia of Theology* (New York: Herder & Herder, 1969), IV, 404-19.

22. St. Thomas's basic analysis of the notion of person and its theological implications can be found in *Summa Theologiae* I, qq. 29-43; *De Potentia* q. 9; *De Unione Verbi Incarnati*. See also U. Degl' Innocenti, O.P., *Il problema della persona nel pensiero di S. Tommaso* (Rome: Pontificia Università Lateranense, 1967); J. Reichman,

"St. Thomas, Capreolus, Cajetan, and the Created Person," *New Scholasicism* 33 (1959), 1-31; 202-30. St. Thomas speaks often of (existing) man as master of himself (*dominus sui*) through his free will: *Summa Theologiae* I-II, q. 6, art. 2 ad 2; II-II, q. 64, art. 5, ad 3; *De Veritate* q. 5, art. 10.

23. *Summa Theologiae* I, q. 29, art. 3.

24. *Sacramentum Mundi* (see note 21), p. 404.

25. See note 22.

26. Cf. J. Etzwiler, "Man as Embodied Spirit," *New Scholasticism* 54 (1980), 358-77; G. Verbeke, "Man as a 'Frontier' according to Aquinas," in G. Verbeke & D. Verhelst, eds., *Aquinas and Problems of His Time* (Leuven: Leuven University Press, 1976), 195-223; A. Pegis, *St. Thomas and the Unity of Man*, in J. McWilliams, ed., *Progress in Philosophy* (Milwaukee: Bruce, 1955), 153-76.

27. *Summa Theologiae* I. q. 12, art., 12; q. 43, art. 7.

28. On the innate dynamism of the human spirit toward the Infinite, cf. my book, *The Philosophical Approach to God* (Winston-Salem: Wake Forest University Publications, 1980), Chap. 1; J. O'Mahoney, *The Desire of God in the Philosophy of St. Thomas* (Cork-Dublin: University of Cork, 1929); B. Lonergan, "The Natural Desire to See God," in *Collection* (New York: Herder & Herder, 1967), 84-95.

29. See the article of Verbeke, "Man as a 'Frontier,'" cited in n. 26.

30. Cf. E. Fackenheim, *Metaphysics and Historicity* (Milwaukee: Marquette University Press, 1960); A. Maurer, *St. Thomas and Historicity* (Milwaukee: Marquette University Press, 1979).

31. *De Veritate* q. 1, art. 9.

32. *Summa contra Gentes* II, chap. 66.

33. John Macmurray, *Persons in Relation* (London: Faber and Faber, 1961).

34. Cf. *De Divisione Naturae*, I, 11, in Thomas Tomasic, "Negative Theology and Subjectivity," *International Philosophical Quarterly* 9 (1969), 411. See also the suggestive work of F. Ulrich, *Homo Abyssus* (1962).

35. Cf. *Summa Theologiae* I, q. 87, art. 1; *De Veritate* q. 10, art. 8 ad 8.

36. St. Thomas develops this idea in the Proemium to *Summa Theologiae* I-II, on the return of man to God through the moral life.

37. Cf. the interesting text of St. Thomas in his *Expositio in Pauli Apostoli Epistolas: In II Cor. 3: 17-18*: "Whoever acts of his own accord acts freely, but one who is impelled by another is not free. He who avoids evil, not because it is evil, but because a precept of the Lord prohibits it, is not free. On the other hand, he who avoids evil because it is evil is free."

38. *De Veritate* q. 17, art. 5 ad 4.

39. Karol Wojtyla, "The Structure of Self-Determination as the Core of the Theory of the Person," in *Tommaso d'Aquino nel suo VII Centennario*, Congresso Internazionale Roma-Napoli (Roma: Edizioni Domenicane Italiane, 1974), 40.

40. Mary Clark, R.S.C.J., "The Personalism of Karol Wotyla," Unpublished Lecture to Personalist Discussion Group, Philadelphia, 1988, pp. 2, 26.

41. Charles Taylor, *Sources of the Self: The Making of the Modern Identity* (Harvard: Harvard University Press, 1988), Part I.

42. John F. Crosby, "The Dialectic of Selfhood and Relatedness in the Human Person," *Proceedings of American Catholic Philosophical Association* (Washington, 1992).

43. Karl Rahner, *Foundations of Christian Faith* (New York: Seabury, 1978), pp. 30-31.

44. *Summa Theoloigae* q. 114, art. 2 ad 1.

45. Cf. e.g., Martin Buber, *I and Thou* (New York: Scribner, 1961); E. Mounier, *Personalism* (New York: Grove, 1952); John Macmurray, *Persons in Relation* (London: Faber & Faber, 1961); Arthur Luther, "Marcel's Metaphysics of the 'We Are,'" *Philosophy Today* 10 (1966), 190-203; Andrew Tallon, "Person and Community: Buber's Category of the Between," ibid. 17 (1973), 62-83; J. Lotz, *Ich-Du-Wir: Fragen um den Menschen* (Frankfurt a/M: Knecht, 1968).

46. Josef Pieper, *The Truth of All Things*, p. 83.

47. John Macmurray, *Persons in Relation* (London: Faber & Faber, 1961).

48. *De Veritate* q. 1, art. 9.

49. Charles Davis, *Body as Spirit* (New York: Seabury, 1979), p. 70.

50. Jacques Maritain, *Existence and the Existent* (Garden City: Doubleday, 1957), p. 90.

51. Jacques Maritain, *Challenges and Renewals* (Notre Dame: University of Notre Dame Press, 1966), pp. 74-75.

52. Norbert Hoffman, *Towards a Civilization of Love* (San Francisco: Ignatius Press, 1985), pp. 237-38, quoted in the interesting article by Robert Connor, "Relation, the Thomistic *Esse*, and American Culture: Toward a Metaphysic of Sanctity," *Communio* 17 (1990), 455-64.

53. Mary Rousseau, *Community: The Tie That Binds*, ch. 4: "The Range of Community." See also the remarkable book of the Greek Orthodox theologian, John D. Zizioulas, *Being as Communion* (Creatwood, NY: St. Vladimir's Seminary Press, 1985). Drawing upon the Trinitarian metaphysics of the Greek Fathers, he concludes that being *is* communion.

54. Cf. *Summa contra Gentes* III, ch. 81; *Summa Theologiae* I, q. 65, art. 2. See the rich development with other texts in Oliva Blanchette, *The Perfection of the Universe according to Aquinas* (University Park: Penn State Univ. Press, 1992), ch. 7: "The Order of Reason and Intelligence: Communication and Knowledge as Ultimate Perfection."

55. On the intellect, see *De Veritate* q. 2, art. 2; on the will, see *De Caritate* art. 7, and Blanchette, pp. 317-19.

56. Karl Rahner, *Christian Commitment* (New York: Sheed and Ward, 1966), pp. 77-78.

57. Gerard O'Hanlon, "Does God Change? Hans Urs von Balthasar on the Immutability of God," *Irish Theological Quarterly* 53 (1987), 161-83, p. 171.

58. Cf. Gerard O'Hanlon, article cited in n. 57 above, and his book, *The Immutability of God in the Theology of Hans Urs von Balthasar* (New York: Cambridge University Press, 1990). A key text of von Balthasar himself is this from *Theodramatik* (Einsiedeln: Johannes Verlag, 1983), IV, 75: "Receiving (*Empfangen*) and letting be (*Geschehenlassen*) are as essential for the concept of absolute love as giving (*das Geben*) which without the receptive letting be – and everything else which belongs to love: the grateful owing of oneself and the turning back of oneself to the giver – would have no capacity to give at all."

59. *Summa contra Gentes* II, ch. 79, 94.

60. *Summa Theologiae* I, q. 77, art. 1 ad 7.

61. *Summa contra Gentes* III, ch. 26; I, ch. 45.

62. Equivalently, when he speaks of our loving God more than self: *Summa Theologiae* I, q. 60, art. 5; I-II, q. 109, art. 3; II-II, q. 26, art. 3.

63. Thomas Berry, *Dreaming the Earth* (San Francisco: Sierra Club, 1988), p. 198.

64. Cf. Robert Johann, *The Meaning of Love* (New York: Paulist, 1966); Raymond McGinnis, *The Wisdom of Love. A Study in the Psycho-Metaphysics of Love according to the Principles of St. Thomas* (Rome: Officium Libri Catholici, 1951).

65. Cf. *In I Sent.*, d. 14, q. 2, art. 2: "In the emergence of creatures from their first source is revealed a kind of circulation (*circulatio*), in which all things return, as to their end, back to the very place from which they had their origin in the first place."

66. Bernard Lonergan, "Christology Today: Methodological Reflections," in *A Third Collection* (New York: Paulist, 1985), p. 77.

67. Thus Ibn Arabi, the Sufi mystic, describes the passing away of the ego-self in the contemplation of the divine beloved through the image of the polished mirror: when the self "passes away" the heart of the devotee becomes like a perfectly polished mirror, so that the mirror itself is no longer seen, but only the image of the divine beloved. Cf. Michael Sells, "Ibn Arabi's Polished Mirror: Perspective Shift and Meaning Event," *Studia Islamica*, forthcoming.

68. Louis Dupré, *Transcendent Selfhood* (New York: Seabury, 1976), where he makes this point, that "it is the nature of the self to be always more than itself."

The Aquinas Lectures
Published by the Marquette University Press
Milwaukee, Wisconsin 53233
United States of America

= =

#1   **St. Thomas and the Life of Learning.** John F. McCormick, S.J. (1937).

ISBN 0-87462-101-1

#2   **St. Thomas and the Gentiles.** Mortimer J. Adler (1938).
ISBN 0-87462-102-X

#3   **St. Thomas and the Greeks.** Anton C. Pegis (1939).
ISBN 0-87462-103-8

#4   **The Nature and Functions of Authority.** Yves Simon (1940).
ISBN 0-87462-104-6

#5   **St. Thomas and Analogy.** Gerald B. Phelan (1941).
ISBN 0-87462-105-4

#6   **St. Thomas and the Problem of Evil.** Jacques Maritain (1942).

ISBN 0-87462-106-2

#7   **Humanism and Theology.** Werner Jaeger (1943).
ISBN 0-87462-107-0

#8   **The Nature and Origins of Scientism.** John Wellmuth (1944).
ISBN 0-87462-108-9

#9   **Cicero in the Courtroom of St. Thomas Aquinas.** E. K. Rand (1945).

ISBN 0-87462-109-7

#10   **St. Thomas and Epistemology.** Louis Marie Regis, O.P. (1946).

ISBN 0-87462-110-0

#50   **Imagination and Metaphysics in St. Augustine.** Robert J.
       O'Connell, S.J. (1986).

                                               ISBN 0-87462-227-1
#51   **Expectations of Immortality in Late Antiquity.** A. Hilary
       Armstrong (1987).

                                               ISBN 0-87462-154-2

#52.   **The Self.** Anthony Kenny (1988).

                                               ISBN 0-87462-155-0

#53.   **The Nature of Philosophical Inquiry.** Quentin P. Lauer, S.J.
       (1989).

                                               ISBN 0-87462-156-9

#54.   **First Principles, Final Ends and Contemporary Philosophical
       Issues.** Alasdair MacIntyre (1990).

                                               ISBN 0-87462-157-7

#55.   **Descartes Among the Scholastics.** Marjorie Grene (1991).
                                               ISBN 0-87462-158-5

#56.   **The Inference That Makes Science.** Ernan McMullin (1992).
                                               ISBN 0-87462-159-3

#57.   **Person and Being.** W. Norris Clarke, S. J.
                                               ISBN 0-87462-160-7

Uniform format, cover, and binding.

Copies of this Aquinas Lecture and the others in the series are
       obtainable from:

                     Marquette University Press
                      Marquette University
                 Milwaukee, Wisconsin 53233, U.S.A.

Publishers of: *Medieval Philosophical Texts in Translation
                     *Pere Marquette Theology Lectures
                     *St. Thomas Aquinas Lectures
                     *Philosophy & Theology (journal)